Learn Java by Examples

Programming examples on almost all the topics of Core Java

Dr T.N.Sharma

Puneet Sharma

ISBN:1493631942
ISBN-13: 9781493631940

CONTENTS
CORE JAVA QUESTIONS

PREFACE

Java is a high-level programming language developed by Sun Microsystems. Java was originally called OAK, and was designed for handheld devices and set-top boxes. Oak was unsuccessful so in 1995 Sun changed the name to Java and modified the language to take advantage of the burgeoning World Wide Web. Java is an object-oriented language similar to C++, but simplified to eliminate language features that cause common programming errors. Java source code files (files with a .java extension) are compiled into a format called bytecode (files with a .class extension), which can then be executed by a Java interpreter. Compiled Java code can run on most computers because Java interpreters and runtime environments, known as Java Virtual Machines (VMs), exist for most operating systems, including UNIX, the Macintosh OS, and Windows. Bytecode can also be converted directly into machine language instructions by a just-in-time compiler (JIT).

Java is a general purpose programming language with a number of features that make the language well suited for use on the World Wide Web. Small Java applications are called Java applets and can be downloaded from a Web server and run on your computer by a Java-compatible Web browser, such as Netscape Navigator or Microsoft Internet Explorer.

These days java is one of the most famous general purpose programming language which are being taught in almost all the computer related studies like BCA, MCA, B.Tech etc. A number of books are available in the market for learning the aspects of java. This book is written exclusively for programming problems. Programming problems for different topics of core java are collected and presented in this book. A good combination of solved and unsolved programming questions are given here. Readers are expected to solve the unsolved questions of their own. Even if, they feel any trouble, the can contact the authors on mail id **tnsharma@logicpace.com and logicpace@gmail.com**.

Chapter 1 deals with introduction of running a small program in java. Also a lots of solved questions related to language fundamentals, operators, arrays and control statements are given here.

In chapter 2, practical problems about classes and related issues are given. Chapter 3 is having questions related to inheritance. Chapter 4 deals with questions of interfaces.

In chapter 5, solved and unsolved programming questions related to exception handling is given whereas chapter 6 deals with string related issues. Chapter 7 is dedicated for problems related to object and wrapper classes. Multithreading is generally a tough issue for first time learners of java. In chapter 8, good questions related to multithreading is given. Questions related to collection and map framework are given in chapter 9. Chapter 10 is dedicated to questions related to input and output.

In last chapter 11, a lots of good examples related user interfaces are given. Almost all the aspects of UI design and AWT are covered in these examples.

1 FUNDAMENAL QUESTION

Running a program in Java

When a program is compiled (e.g. C or C++ program), it is directly translated into machine code that is specific to a platform/processor. But running a Java program is a two-step process. In Java translation from source code to the executable code is achieved using two translators:

Java Compiler: A Java program is first compiled by the Java Compiler to generate bytecode. Bytecode resemble machine code but it is not specific to any platform i.e. it can not be executed on a computer without further translation.

Java Interpreter: Java Interpreter executes the bytecode after interpreting and converting into machine code. In the newer versions of Java, JIT (Just in time) compiler is also added to JRE for this purpose.

Java programs run at a slower speed as compared to C/C++ programs as bytecode is interpreted during each run while in case of C/C++, source code is compiled only once into the executable code, which then runs directly on the hardware.

In order to write and run a Java program we need an editor, Java Compiler and a Java Runtime Environment.

The editor can be any text editor like Notepad, WordPad, Edit etc. The easiest way to get a Java Compiler and Runtime Environment is to download and install Sun's Java Development Kit (**JDK**).

Although we have not discussed the syntax of the language so far but to understand the process of running a Java program we will discuss a simple program.

Example: The following Java program just displays the message "Hello World" on the monitor/console.

Step1:   The Java program should be written in a text file with the extension "**.java**". You already know that a C program is written into a text file with "**.C**" extension and a C++ program is normally written into a text file with "**.CPP**" extension.

Write the following code into file "**Hello.java**" using any text editor:

```
public class Hello
{
  public static void main(String args[])
   {
       System.out.println("Hello World");
   }
}
```

Note: Java is a case-sensitive language like C/C++ so you should be very careful about the case while writing Java programs.

<u>Step 2</u>: Compile the Java program written above using the command:

    javac Hello.java

    The java source code will be compiled into bytecode, which will be stored in file "**Hello.class**".

<u>Step 3</u>: Run the java program compiled above using the command:

    java Hello

    On successful execution the following message will be displayed on the console/monitor:

    Hello World

<u>Note</u>:   The JDK must be installed on the machine before you can compile and run the Java program. If you install the JDK in folder **c:\jdk\bin** then this folder must be in the "PATH" so that you can compile and run your Java program from any folder. Give the following command in the command window from which you want to compile and run the Java program:

   SET PATH=%PATH%;C:\JDK\BIN;

General Problem Set This is general set of programs related to simple programming constructs and fundamental of java language

Q1.Write a program, which reads two numbers by command line arguments and displays their sum.

Solution

```java
class TwoNumSum
    {
        public static void main(String args[])
        {
          int length;
          length = args.length;
          if (length != 2)
              System.out.println("Provide two integer numbers");
          else
            {
            int n1 = Integer.parseInt(args[0]);
            int n2 = Integer.parseInt(args[1]);
            int n= n1+n2;
            System.out.println("Sum = "+n);
            }
        }
}
```

Q2. Write a program, which reads two numbers from user and displays their product.

Solution

```java
import java.io.*;
class TwoNumProduct
{
    public static void main(String args[]) throws IOException
    {
  BufferedReader input = new BufferedReader(new InputStreamReader(System.in));
    int n1 = 0, n2 = 0, Product = 0;
      String inputValue;
      System.out.print("Enter First Number :");
      inputValue = input.readLine();
      n1 = Integer.parseInt(inputValue);
      System.out.print("Enter Second Number :");
      inputValue = input.readLine();
      n2= Integer.parseInt(inputValue);
      Product= n1 * n2;
      System.out.println("Two Number Product is : = "+Product);
    }
}
```

Q3. Write a program to calculate the area and circumference of a given circle.

Solution

```java
import java.io.*;
class Circle
{
    public static void main(String args[]) throws IOException
    {
        BufferedReader input = new BufferedReader(new
        InputStreamReader(System.in));
            double radious,area,circumfr;
            String inputValue;
        System.out.print("Enter The radious of the Circle: = ");
        inputValue = input.readLine();
        radious = Double.parseDouble(inputValue);
        area = Math.PI * radious * radious;
        circumfr = 2 * Math.PI * radious;
        System.out.println("The Area of the Circle is: = "+area);
    System.out.println("The Circumference of the Circle is: = "+circumfr);
    }
    }
```

Q4. Write a program to find the larger of the two given numbers.

Solution
```java
import java.io.*;
class LargerNumber
{
    public static void main(String args[]) throws IOException
    {
BufferedReader input = new BufferedReader(new InputStreamReader(System.in));
String inputValue;
        System.out.print("Enter The First Value to Check Largest A: ");
    inputValue = input.readLine();
    int first = Integer.parseInt(inputValue);
    System.out.print("Enter The Second Value to Check Largest B: ");
    inputValue = input.readLine();
    int second = Integer.parseInt(inputValue);
     if(first>second)
    { System.out.println(first+" is Larger Then "+second);
    }
    else
    {
        if(first<second)
        { System.out.println(second+" is Larger Then "+first);
        }
        else
        { System.out.println("Both are equal");
        }
    }
    }
}
```

Q5.Write a program to find the largest of the three given numbers.

Solution
```java
import java.io.*;
class LargestOfThree
{
    public static void main(String args[]) throws IOException
    {
        BufferedReader input = new BufferedReader(new InputStreamReader(System.in));
    String inputValue;
        System.out.print("Enter The First Value: ");
        inputValue = input.readLine();
        int first = Integer.parseInt(inputValue);
        System.out.print("Enter The Second Value: ");
        inputValue = input.readLine();
        int second = Integer.parseInt(inputValue);
        System.out.print("Enter The Third Value: ");
    inputValue = input.readLine();
```

```java
int third = Integer.parseInt(inputValue);

if(first>second)
{   if(first>third)
    { System.out.println(first+" is Largest");
    }
    else
    { System.out.println(third+" is Largest");
    }
}
else
{

    if(second>third)
    { System.out.println(second+" is Largest");
    }
    else
    { System.out.println(third+" is Largest");
    }

}
    }
}
```

Q6. Write a program to find the second largest of the three given numbers.
Solution

```java
import java.io.*;
class SecondLargest
{
    public static void main(String args[]) throws IOException
    { BufferedReader input = new BufferedReader(new InputStreamReader(System.in));
        String inputValue;
        System.out.print("Enter The First Value: ");
    inputValue = input.readLine();
    int first = Integer.parseInt(inputValue);
    System.out.print("Enter The Second Value: ");
    inputValue = input.readLine();
    int second = Integer.parseInt(inputValue);
    System.out.print("Enter The Third Value: ");
    inputValue = input.readLine();
    int third = Integer.parseInt(inputValue);
     if (first > second)
     {
        if(first<third)
        {System.out.println(first+" is Second Largest Number");
        }
        else
        {
            if(second>third)
            {System.out.println(second+" is Second Largest Number");
            }
            else
```

```
                {System.out.println(third+" is Second Largest Number");
                }
            }
        }
        else
        {
            if(second < third)
                {System.out.println(second+" is Second Largest Number");
                }
            else
                {
                    if(first>second)
                    {System.out.println(first+" is Second Largest Number");
                    }
                    else
                    {System.out.println(third+" is Second largest Number");
                    }
                }
        }
    }
}
```

Q7. Write a program to calculate the DA for a given basic salary using following rules.
a. BASIC <= 5500 THEN DA = 155% of BASIC SALARY.
b. BASIC > 5500 AND BASIC <= 8000 THEN DA = 155% of the 5500 or 119% of the BASIC
      whichever is higher.
c. OTHERWISE DA = 119% OF 8000 or 103% of the BASIC whichever is higher.

Solution
```
import java.io.*;
class CalculateDA
{
    public static void main(String args[]) throws IOException
    {
    BufferedReader input = new BufferedReader(new InputStreamReader(System.in));
String inputValue;
    float DA=0,BasicSalary=0;
    System.out.print("Enter Your Basic Salary:= ");
    inputValue = input.readLine();
    BasicSalary = Float.parseFloat(inputValue);
    if (BasicSalary <= 5500)
    {
        DA = BasicSalary * 155/100;
    }
    else if(BasicSalary<=8000)
    {   if(5500*155/100 > BasicSalary*119/100)
        {
            DA = 5500 * 155/100;
        }
        else
```

```java
        {
            DA = BasicSalary * 119/100;
        }
    }
    else
    {
        if(8000*119/100 > BasicSalary*103/100)
        {
            DA = 8000*119/100;
        }
        else
        {
            DA = BasicSalary*103/100;
        }
    }
    System.out.println("Your Basic Salary is :=  "+ BasicSalary);
    System.out.println("DA according to your Basic Salary is:= " +DA);
    }
}
```

Q8. Write a program to find the roots of a quadratic equation $ax^2 + bx + c = 0$

Solution

```java
import java.io.*;
class QuadraticRoot
{
    public static void main(String args[]) throws IOException
    {
    BufferedReader input = new BufferedReader(new InputStreamReader(System.in));  String inputValue;
    System.out.print("Enter The Value of a: ");
     inputValue = input.readLine();
     double a = Double.parseDouble(inputValue);
     System.out.print("Enter The Value of b: ");
     inputValue = input.readLine();
     double b = Double.parseDouble(inputValue);
     System.out.print("Enter The Value of c: ");
inputValue = input.readLine();
     double c = Double.parseDouble(inputValue);
     double x =(b*b)-4*a*c;
     double disc = Math.sqrt(x);
     if(disc>0)
     {
         double root1=(-b+disc)/(2*a);
         double root2=(-b-disc)/(2*a);
         System.out.println("The Quadradic Equation roots are root1:= "+root1 +"
       and root2:= "+root2);
     }
     else if(disc==0)
     {
         double root=-b/(2*a);
```

```
        System.out.println("Both roots are Equal & value is := "+root);
    }
    else
    {
        System.out.println("The Value of (b^2-4ac) is Less then Zero");
    }
  }
}
```

Q9 Write a program, which reads an integer number and calculates sum of its digits.

Solution
```
import java.io.*;
class SumOfDigits
{
    public static void main(String args[]) throws IOException
    {
    BufferedReader input = new BufferedReader(new InputStreamReader(System.in));
    String inputValue;
    int sum=0,mod=1;
      System.out.print("Enter an Integer Number:= ");
      inputValue = input.readLine();
      int num = Integer.parseInt(inputValue);
      int num1;
      if(num<0)
          num1=-num;
    else
          num1=num;
      while(num1>0)
      {
          mod=num1%10;
          num1=num1/10;
          sum=sum+mod;
      }
      System.out.println("Sum of Digits:= " +sum);
    }
}
```

Q10. Write a program, which reads an integer number and generates a new number in which order of the digits is reversed.

Solution
```
import java.io.*;
class ReverseIntegerNum
{
    public static void main(String args[]) throws IOException
    {
    BufferedReader input = new BufferedReader(new InputStreamReader(System.in));
    String inputValue;
    int rev=0,mod=1;
```

```java
        System.out.print("Enter the Integer number to be reversed:=  ");
        inputValue = input.readLine();
        int num = Integer.parseInt(inputValue);
        int sign;
        if(num<0)
            sign=-1;
        else
            sign=1;
        int num1=num*sign;
        while(num1>0)
          {
            mod=num1%10;
            num1=num1/10;
            rev=10*rev+mod;
          }
        System.out.println("The reversed number is:= " +rev*sign);
      }
}
```

Q11 Write a program, which finds the factorial of a given number.

Solution
```java
import java.io.*;
class Factorial
{
     public static void main(String args[]) throws IOException
       {
     BufferedReader input = new BufferedReader(new InputStreamReader(System.in));
     String inputValue;
     long fact=1;
        System.out.print("Enter The Integer Number:=  ");
        inputValue = input.readLine();
        int num = Integer.parseInt(inputValue);
        if(num<0)
          {
            System.out.println("Enter The Positive Number");
            System.exit(111);
          }
        for(int i=1; i<=num; i++)
          {
            fact = fact*i;
          }
        System.out.println("The Factorial of " +num +" = " + fact);
      }
}
```
-------------------------------------- or --------------------------------------
```java
// Factorial using Recursion
import java.io.*;
class FactorialFun
{
```

```java
    long Fact(int n)
    {
       if(n==0 || n==1)
          return 1;
       else
          return n*Fact(n-1);
    }
}
class FindFactorial
{
    public static void main(String args[]) throws IOException
    {
       BufferedReader input = new BufferedReader(new InputStreamReader(System.in));
    String inputValue;
    int sum=0,mod=1,mul=1;
       System.out.print("Enter The Number:=  ");
       inputValue = input.readLine();
       int num = Integer.parseInt(inputValue);
       if(num<0)
       {
          System.out.println("Enter The Positive Number");
          System.exit(-55);
       }
       FactorialFun f = new FactorialFun();
       System.out.println("Factorial of " +num +" = " +f.Fact(num));
    }
}
```

Q12. Write a program, which generates the N terms of the Fibonacci series.
Solution

```java
import java.io.*;
class FibonacciSeries
{
    public static void main(String args[]) throws IOException
    {
    BufferedReader input = new BufferedReader(new InputStreamReader(System.in));
    String inputValue;
    int num=0,a=0,b=1,c=0;
       System.out.print("Enter the number of terms:=  ");
       inputValue = input.readLine();
       num = Integer.parseInt(inputValue);
       System.out.print("The Fibonacii series  is: ");
       for(int i=1;i<=num;i++)
       {
          System.out.print(a +", ");
          c=a+b;
          a=b;
          b=c;
       }
       System.out.println();
```

```
        }
    }
```

Q13. Write a program, which checks whether a given number is prime or not and displays an appropriate message.
Solution

```java
import java.io.*;
class CheckPrimeNumber
{
    public static void main(String args[]) throws IOException
    {
    BufferedReader input = new BufferedReader(new InputStreamReader(System.in));
    String inputValue;
    boolean flag=false;
    int num=0,i=0;
        System.out.print("Give The Number to be checked:  ");
        inputValue = input.readLine();
        num = Integer.parseInt(inputValue);
        double sqrtnum =Math.sqrt(num);
        for(i=2;i<sqrtnum;i++)
        {   if(num%i==0)
            {
                flag=true;
                break;
            }
        }
        if(flag)
        {
            System.out.println("The given number is not a prime Number!");
        }
        else
        {
            System.out.println("The given number is a prime Number!");
        }
    }
}
```

Q14 Write a program, which reads two integer numbers and displays their L.C.M.
Solution

```java
import java.io.*;
    class CalculateLCM
    {
    public static void main(String args[]) throws IOException
    {
    BufferedReader input = new BufferedReader(new InputStreamReader(System.in));
    String inputValue;
    int n1=0,n2=0,i=0,n=1,lcm;
    System.out.print("Enter The First Number:= ");
      inputValue = input.readLine();
```

```java
        n1 = Integer.parseInt(inputValue);
        System.out.print("Enter The Second Number:= ");
        inputValue = input.readLine();
        n2 = Integer.parseInt(inputValue);
        int a = n1;
        int b = n2;
        while(n1!=0 && n2!=0)
        {
            if(n1>n2)
            {
                n1=n1%n2;
            }
            else
            {
                n2=n2%n1;
            }
        }
        if(n1==0)
            lcm=a*b/n2;
        else
            lcm=a*b/n1;
        System.out.print("The LCM of Given Two Number is:= " +lcm);
        System.out.println();
    }
}
```

Q15. Write a program to read and write an array.

Solution
```java
import java.io.*;
class RWArray
{
    public static void main(String args[]) throws IOException
    {
    BufferedReader input = new BufferedReader(new InputStreamReader(System.in));
    String inputValue;
      System.out.print("Enter The Size of an Array: = ");
      inputValue = input.readLine();
    int size = Integer.parseInt(inputValue);
    int Array [] = new int[size];
      for(int i=0; i<size; i++)
      {
          System.out.print("Enter the element Array["+i +"] := ");
          inputValue = input.readLine();
          int element = Integer.parseInt(inputValue);
          Array[i]=element;
      }
    System.out.println("The array elements are as follows:");
    for(int i=0; i<size; i++)
    {
```

```java
      System.out.println("Array["+i+"] = " + Array[i]);
    }
  }
}
```

Q16. Write a program to find the sum and average of N given numbers.

Solution
```java
import java.io.*;
class SumAverageArray
{
    public static void main(String args[]) throws IOException
    {
    BufferedReader input = new BufferedReader(new InputStreamReader(System.in));
    String inputValue;
      System.out.print("Enter the size of array: = ");
      inputValue = input.readLine();
    int size = Integer.parseInt(inputValue);
    int array [] = new int[size];
      int sum=0;
      float average=0;
      for(int i=0; i<size; i++)
      {   System.out.print("Enter the number at array["+i +"] := ");
          inputValue = input.readLine();
          int element = Integer.parseInt(inputValue);
          array[i]=element;
      }
      System.out.println("The array elements are as follows:");
      for(int i=0; i<size; i++)
      {
          System.out.println("array["+i+"] = " + array[i]);
          sum=sum+array[i];
      }
      average = (float)sum/size;
      System.out.println("The Sum of the Array Element is := " +sum);
      System.out.println("The Average of the Array Element is := " +average);
    }
}
```

Q17.Write a program, which deletes an element whose position is specified from an array.

Solution
```java
import java.io.*;
class DeleteElement
{
    public static void main(String args[]) throws IOException
    {
        BufferedReader input = new BufferedReader(new InputStreamReader(System.in));
        String inputValue;
        int position=0;
```

```java
System.out.print("Enter the No. of elements in array: = ");
inputValue = input.readLine();
 int size = Integer.parseInt(inputValue);
 int Array [] = new int[100];
 for(int i=0; i<size; i++)
    {
        System.out.print("Enter The Element at Array["+i +"] := ");
        inputValue = input.readLine();
        int element = Integer.parseInt(inputValue);
    Array[i]=element;
 }
System.out.println("The Array Elements are as Follows:");
for(int i=0; i<size; i++)
 {
     System.out.println("Array["+i+"] = " + Array[i]);
 }
System.out.print("Enter the position of the element to be deleted:= ");
 inputValue = input.readLine();
position = Integer.parseInt(inputValue);
 if(position < size)
 {   for(int i=position; i<=size; i++)
     {    Array[i] = Array[i+1];
     }
 }
 size=size-1;
 System.out.println("The array after deletion is as follows:");
 for(int i=0; i<size; i++)
 {   System.out.println("Array["+i+"] = " + Array[i]);
 }
    }
 }
```

Q18. Write a program, which inserts a given element at a specific location in an array.

Solution
```java
import java.io.*;
class InsertElement
{
    public static void main(String args[]) throws IOException
    {
    BufferedReader input = new BufferedReader(new InputStreamReader(System.in));
    String inputValue;
     int position = 0;
     int value = 0;
     System.out.print("Enter the No. of elements in array: = ");
      inputValue = input.readLine();
    int size = Integer.parseInt(inputValue);
    int Array [] = new int[100];
     for(int i=0; i<size; i++)
     {   System.out.print("Enter The Element at Array["+i +"] := ");
```

```
            inputValue = input.readLine();
            int element = Integer.parseInt(inputValue);
            Array[i]=element;
        }
      System.out.println("The Array Elements are as Follows:");
      for(int i=0; i<size; i++)
      {   System.out.println("Array["+i+"] = " + Array[i]);
      }
      System.out.print("Enter the position at which element is to be inserted:= ");
inputValue = input.readLine();
position = Integer.parseInt(inputValue);
        System.out.print("Enter the value of the element to be inserted:= ");
        inputValue = input.readLine();
      value = Integer.parseInt(inputValue);
      for(int i = size; i > position; i--)
            Array[i] = Array[i-1];
        Array[position] = value;
        size=size+1;
        System.out.println("The Array After Insertion is as Follows:");
        for(int i=0; i<size; i++)
        {   System.out.println("Array["+i+"] = " + Array[i]);
        }
      }
    }
}
```

Q19. Write a program to sort the N given numbers using bubble sort method.

Solution
```
import java.io.*;
class BubbleSort
{
    public static void main(String args[]) throws IOException
        {
        BufferedReader input = new BufferedReader(new InputStreamReader(System.in));
        String inputValue;
        int position = 0;
        int value = 0;
        System.out.print("Enter The Size of Array: = ");
        inputValue = input.readLine();
        int size = Integer.parseInt(inputValue);
        int Array [] = new int[size];
        for(int i=0; i<size; i++)
            {
                System.out.print("Enter The Element: ");
                inputValue = input.readLine();
                int element = Integer.parseInt(inputValue);
                Array[i]=element;
            }
            for(int i = 0; i < size-1; i++)
```

```java
        {
            for(int j=0; j < size-(i+1);j++)
            {
                if(Array[j] > Array[j+1])
                {
                    int temp= Array[j];
                    Array[j] = Array[j+1];
                    Array[j+1] = temp;
                }
            }
        }
        System.out.println("Array Elements After the Bubble Sort:");
        for(int i=0; i<size; i++)
        {
            System.out.println(Array[i]);
        }
    }
}
```

Q20. Write a program to read and write a matrix.
Solution

```java
import java.io.*;
class RWMatrix
{
    public static void main(String args[]) throws IOException
    {
    BufferedReader input = new BufferedReader(new InputStreamReader(System.in));
    String inputValue;
      System.out.print("Enter The Row Size: = ");
      inputValue = input.readLine();
    int row = Integer.parseInt(inputValue);
    System.out.print("Enter The Column Size: = ");
      inputValue = input.readLine();
      int column = Integer.parseInt(inputValue);
      int mat [][] = new int[row][column];
      for(int i=0; i<row; i++)
      {
       for(int j=0; j<column; j++)
       {
           System.out.print("Enter The Element at position:["+i +"]["+j +"] :=");
           inputValue = input.readLine();
           int element = Integer.parseInt(inputValue);
           mat[i][j]=element;
       }
      }
      System.out.println("Your Matrix is as Follows: = ");
      for(int i=0; i<row; i++)
      {
          for(int j=0; j<column; j++)
          {
```

```
                System.out.print(mat[i][j] +" ");
            }
        System.out.println();
        }
    }
}


Q21. Write a program to find the transpose of a given matrix.
```

Solution

```
import java.io.*;
class Transpose
{
    public static void main(String args[]) throws IOException
    {
    BufferedReader input = new BufferedReader(new InputStreamReader(System.in));
    String inputValue;

        System.out.print("Enter The Row Size: = ");
        inputValue = input.readLine();
    int row = Integer.parseInt(inputValue);

        System.out.print("Enter The Column Size: = ");
        inputValue = input.readLine();
        int column = Integer.parseInt(inputValue);

    int mat [][] = new int[row][column];
        int transmat [][] = new int[column][row];

        for(int i=0; i<row; i++)
        {
            for(int j=0; j<column; j++)
            {
                System.out.print("Enter The Element at position:["+i +"]["+j +"] :=");
                inputValue = input.readLine();
                int element = Integer.parseInt(inputValue);
                mat[i][j]=element;
            }
        }
        System.out.println("Your given Matrix is as Follows");
        for(int i=0; i<row; i++)
        {
            for(int j=0; j<column; j++)
            {
                transmat[j][i] = mat[i][j];
                System.out.print(mat[i][j] +" ");
            }
            System.out.println();
        }
        System.out.println("The Transpose of the Given Matrix is as Follows");
        for(int i=0; i<column; i++)
```

```
        {
            for(int j=0; j<row; j++)
            {
               System.out.print(" " + transmat[i][j]);
            }
            System.out.println();
        }
    }
}
```

Q22. Write a program to multiply the two matrices.

Solution

```java
import java.io.*;
class MulTwoMatrix
{
    public static void main(String args[]) throws IOException
    {
    BufferedReader input = new BufferedReader(new InputStreamReader(System.in));
    String inputValue;

      System.out.print("Enter The Row Size of the First Matrix := ");
       inputValue = input.readLine();
    int row1 = Integer.parseInt(inputValue);

    System.out.print("Enter The Column Size of the First Matrix := ");
       inputValue = input.readLine();
       int column1 = Integer.parseInt(inputValue);

       System.out.print("Enter The Row Size of the Second Matrix := ");
        inputValue = input.readLine();
    int row2 = Integer.parseInt(inputValue);

    System.out.print("Enter The Column Size of the Second Matrix := ");
       inputValue = input.readLine();
       int column2 = Integer.parseInt(inputValue);

    if((column1!=row2))
     {
         System.out.println("This Matix can not be multiplied because Column1 and
        row2 are not Same");
         System.exit(-100);
     }
    int matrix1 [][] = new int[row1][column1];
     int matrix2 [][] = new int[row2][column2];
     int mul [][] = new int[row1][column2];

     for(int i=0; i<row1; i++)
     {
         for(int j=0; j<column1; j++)
```

```java
            {
                System.out.print("Enter The First Matrix Element at position:["+i
        +"]["+j +"] :=");
                inputValue = input.readLine();
                int element = Integer.parseInt(inputValue);
                matrix1[i][j]=element;
            }
        }

for(int i=0; i<row2; i++)
        {
            for(int j=0; j<column2; j++)
            {
                System.out.print("Enter The Second Matrix Element at position:["+i
        +"]["+j +"] :=");
                inputValue = input.readLine();
                int element = Integer.parseInt(inputValue);
                matrix2[i][j]=element;
            }
        }
        System.out.println("Your First Matrix is as Follows:");


        for(int i=0; i<row1; i++)
        {
            for(int j=0; j<column1; j++)
                {
                    System.out.print(matrix1[i][j] +" ");
                }
                System.out.println();
        }
        System.out.println("Your Second Matrix is as Follows:");

    for(int i=0; i<row2; i++)
    {
        for(int j=0; j<column2; j++)
        {
            System.out.print(matrix2[i][j] +" ");
        }
        System.out.println();
    }

    System.out.println("The Multiplication of two matrix is as follow \n");
    for(int i=0;i<row1;i++)
    {
        for(int j=0;j<column2;j++)
        {
            mul[i][j]= 0;
            for(int k=0;k<column1;k++)
            {
```

```
            mul[i][j]=mul[i][j] + matrix1[i][k]*matrix2[k][j];
        }
        System.out.print(mul[i][j]+" ");
    }
    System.out.println();
   }
  }
}
```

2 CLASS FUNDAMENTAL

Solved Questions

1. Write a class **Math** to implement the following simple arithmetic operations:
   (a) Addition   (b) Subtraction   (c) Division, and   (d) Multiplication
   Note: All the methods must be static. Also make sure that it should not be possible to instantiate the class.

2. Implement a class **Complex**, which should provide methods to perform the following operations on complex numbers:
   (a) Addition   (b) Subtraction
   Note: Implement using static as well as non-static (instance) methods. Decide whether implementing all the methods as static would be a better alternative in this case.

3. Implement class **Stack.** The class should implement the following operations:
   (i)   void push(int x);
   (ii)   int pop();
   (iii)   int peek()
   (iv)   boolean isStackEmpty()
   (v)   boolean isStackFull()
   (vi)   void display()

   Write a menu-driven program, which makes use of the **Stack** class to create the stack of the desired size. The program should prompt the user to select the desired option and then take appropriate action based on the user choice. The user should also be provided the exit option.
   Note: Repeat the above problem with dynamic implementation of stack.

4. Implement class **Queue.** The class should implement the following operations:
   (i)   void add(int x);
   (ii)   int delete();
   (vii)   boolean isQueueEmpty()
   (viii)   boolean isQueueFull()
   (ix)   void display()

   Write a menu-driven program, which makes use of the Queue class to create the queue of the desired size. The program should prompt the user to select the desired option and then take appropriate action based on the user choice. The user should also be provided the exit option.

Unsolved Programming Questions

5 Repeat the question number 4 with dynamic implementation of queue.

6. Write a program to reverse a given array of numbers using a stack. The size of the stack should be

same as the number of elements in the array.

7. Write class "**ThreeDimObject**" and define overloaded methods named **volume()** to calculate the volumes of various 3D-Objects (cube, cuboid, sphere and cylinder).

8. Write a class **Account** to represent bank account of a customer with the following data members: Name of the depositor, account number, type of account (S for saving, C for current) & balance amount and member methods/constructors to do the following: to initialize data members, to deposit money, to withdraw money after checking the balance (minimum balance is Rs.1000) and to display the data members. Write a program to create an array of **Account** objects to hold account details of 10 customers which would be read from the keyboard. Perform deposit and withdraw operations on some of the accounts and then display the modified details.

Solutions

Q 1. Write a class **Math** to implement the following simple arithmetic operations:
  (a) Addition   (b) Subtraction   (c) Division, and   (d) Multiplication
  Note: All the methods must be static. Also make sure that it should not be possible to instantiate the class.

Solution
File: MyMath.java: The file in which class MyMath is defined.

```java
import java.io.*;
class MyMath {
    private MyMath() {

    }
    public static double divide(double x, double y) {
        return x/y;
    }
    public static double multiply(double x, double y) {
        return x*y;
    }
    public static double subtract(double x, double y) {
        return x-y;
    }
    public static double add(double x, double y) {
        return x+y;
    }
}
```

File: TestMath.java

```java
import java.io.BufferedReader;
```

```java
import java.io.InputStreamReader;
class TestMath {
    public static void main(String[] args) throws Exception{
            double x,y,result; // x, y are two variables representing two numbers and result is
            //representing result getting after performing operation on these two numbers.
        BufferedReader br=new BufferedReader(new InputStreamReader(System.in));
        System.out.print("Enter First Number : ");
        x=Double.parseDouble(br.readLine());
        System.out.print("Enter Second Number : ");
        y=Double.parseDouble(br.readLine());
        result=Math.add(x,y);
        System.out.println("x = "+x+" y = "+y);
        System.out.println("After addition result x+y = "+result);
        result=Math.subtract(x,y);
        System.out.println("After subtraction result x-y = "+result);
        result=Math.multiply(x,y);
        System.out.println("After multiplication result x*y = "+result);
        result=Math.divide(x,y);
        System.out.println("After divide result x/y = "+result);

    }

}
```

Q 2. Implement a class **Complex**, which should provide methods to perform the following operations
on complex numbers:

(a) Addition   (b) Subtraction

Note: Implement using static as well as non-static (instance) methods. Decide whether
implementing all the methods as static would be a better alternative in this case.

Solutions

File: Complex1.java: This class is implemented with non-static methods.

```java
class Complex1
{
    public double realno;
    public double imgno;
    Complex1(){

    }
    Complex1(double r,double i)
    {
        realno=r;
        imgno=i;
    }
    public Complex1 add(Complex1 x, Complex1 y)
    {
        double r = x.realno + y.realno;
        double i = x.imgno + y.imgno;
        return new Complex1(r,i);
    }
```

```java
public Complex1 subtract(Complex1 x, Complex1 y)
{

    double r = x.realno - y.realno;
    double i = x.imgno - y.imgno;
    return new Complex1(r,i);
}
public Complex1 multiply (Complex1 x, Complex1 y)
{
double r2 = x.realno * y.realno - x.imgno * y.imgno;
double i2 = x.imgno  * y.realno + x.realno  * y.imgno;
return new Complex1 (r2, i2);
}


public Complex1 divide (Complex1 x, Complex1 y)
{
double d = y.realno * y.realno + y.imgno  * y.imgno;
double r = x.realno * y.realno + x.imgno  * y.imgno;
double i = x.imgno * y.realno - x.realno * y.imgno;
return new Complex1 (r/d, i/d);
}

public String toString ()
{
String imgsign = (imgno < 0) ? " - " : " + ";
return ("("+realno+") " +  imgsign + "("+imgno + "i)");
}
}
```

File: Complex.java: This class is implemented with static methods.

```java
class Complex
{
    public double realno;
    public double imgno;

    Complex(double r,double i)
    {
        realno=r;
        imgno=i;
    }
    public static Complex add(Complex x, Complex y)
    {
        double r = x.realno + y.realno;
        double i = x.imgno + y.imgno;
        return new Complex(r,i);
    }
    public static Complex subtract(Complex x, Complex y)
    {
        double r = x.realno - y.realno;
```

```java
        double i = x.imgno - y.imgno;
        return new Complex(r,i);
    }
    public static Complex multiply (Complex x, Complex y)
    {
    double r2 = x.realno * y.realno - x.imgno * y.imgno;
    double i2 = x.imgno  * y.realno + x.realno  * y.imgno;
    return new Complex (r2, i2);
    }

    public static Complex divide (Complex x, Complex y)
    {
    double d = y.realno * y.realno + y.imgno  * y.imgno;
    double r = x.realno * y.realno + x.imgno  * y.imgno;
    double i = x.imgno * y.realno - x.realno * y.imgno;
    return new Complex (r/d, i/d);
    }

    public String toString ()
    {
    String imgsign = (imgno < 0) ? " - " : " + ";
    return ("("+realno+") " +  imgsign + "("+imgno + "i)");
    }
}
```

File: TextComplex.java

```java
class TestComplex
{
  public static void main (String [] args)
  {
    //using instance methods
    Complex1 a = new Complex1 (2,3);// first expression (2+3i)
    Complex1 b = new Complex1 (4,6);// second expression (4+6i)
    Complex1 complex1 = new Complex1();
    Complex1 value1 = complex1.add(a,b);
    Complex1 value2 = complex1.subtract (a,b);
    Complex1 value3 = complex1.multiply (a,b);
    Complex1 value4 = complex1.divide (a,b);
    System.out.println("Following result is using instance methods: ");
    System.out.println("Addition : "+value1);
    System.out.println("Subtraction : "+value2);
    System.out.println("Multiplication : "+value3);
    System.out.println("Division : "+value4);

    //using static methods
    Complex x = new Complex (2,3);// first expression (2+3i)
    Complex y = new Complex (4,6);// second expression (4+6i)
    Complex value5 = Complex.add (x,y);
    Complex value6 = Complex.subtract (x,y);
    Complex value7 = Complex.multiply (x,y);
```

```java
Complex value8 = Complex.divide (x,y);
System.out.println("Following result is using static methods: ");
System.out.println("Addition : "+value5);
System.out.println("Subtraction : "+value6);
System.out.println("Multiplication : "+value7);
System.out.println("Division : "+value8);
   }
}
```

Q 3. Implement class **Stack.** The class should implement the following operations:

- (i)   void push(int x);
- (ii)   int pop();
- (iii)   int peek()
- (iv)   boolean isStackEmpty()
- (v)   boolean isStackFull()
- (vi)   void display()

Write a menu-driven program, which makes use of the **Stack** class to create the stack of the desired size. The program should prompt the user to select the desired option and then take appropriate action based on the user choice. The user should also be provided the exit option.

Note: Repeat the above problem with dynamic implementation of stack.

Solution for static stack
Stack.java
```java
class Stack {
    int s[]=new int[20];
    int tos=-1; //top of stack
    int n;      //number of elements

    public Stack(int n) {
        this.n = n;
    }
    public void push(int x) {
        if(isStackFull()) {
            return;
        }
        tos++;
        s[tos]=x;
    }
    public int pop() {
        int value=s[tos];
        tos--;
        return value;
    }
    public int peek() {
        return s[tos];
    }
    public boolean isStackEmpty() {
```

```java
            if(tos < 0) {
                return true;
            }
            return false;
        }
        public boolean isStackFull() {
            if(tos == n-1) {
                return true;
            }
            return false;
        }
        public void display() {
            for(int i=tos; i >= 0; i--) {
                System.out.println("["+s[i]+"]");
            }
        }
    }
}
```

File: TestStack.java

```java
import java.io.BufferedReader;
import java.io.InputStreamReader;

public class TestStack {
    public static void main(String[] args) throws Exception{
        BufferedReader br=new BufferedReader(new InputStreamReader(System.in));//to read from
keyboard
        System.out.print("Enter the size of stack (<= 20) : ");
        int sizeOfStack=Integer.parseInt(br.readLine());
        if (sizeOfStack > 20) {
            System.out.println("Size of stack must be <= 20");
            return;
        }
        Stack stack = new Stack(sizeOfStack);//creating an instance of Stack class
        boolean wantToExit=false;
        do {
            System.out.println();
            System.out.println("[Menu] Press :");
            System.out.println("1 : To push new element into stack.");
            System.out.println("2 : To pop top element from stack.");
            System.out.println("3 : To display peek element.");
            System.out.println("4 : To display all elements of stack.");
            System.out.println("5 : To exit from menu");
            int option=Integer.parseInt(br.readLine());
            switch (option) {
            case 1:
                if(stack.isStackFull()) {
                    System.out.println("You can not push more values: Stack full");
                    break;
                }
                System.out.println("Enter value to push : ");
```

```java
                int value = Integer.parseInt(br.readLine());
                stack.push(value);
                break;
        case 2:
            if(stack.isStackEmpty()) {
                System.out.println("You can not pop value: Stack empty");
                    break;
            }
            int poppedValue = stack.pop();
            System.out.println("The popped value is : "+poppedValue);
            break;
        case 3:
            if(stack.isStackEmpty()) {
                System.out.println("There is no peek value : Stack empty");
                    break;
            }
            int peekValue = stack.peek();
            System.out.println("The peek value is : "+peekValue);
            break;
        case 4:
            if(stack.isStackEmpty()) {
                    System.out.println("Stack empty");
                    break;
            }
            System.out.println("Values in stack are as follows : ");
            stack.display();
            break;
        case 5:
            System.out.println("Bye");
            wantToExit=true;
            break;
        default:
            System.out.println("Invalid option pressed");
            break;
        }

        } while (!wantToExit);
    }
}
```

Solution for dynamic stack
File: Node.java

```java
class Node{
    Node nextNode;
    int value;
}
```

File: DynamicStack.java

```java
class DynamicStack {
```

```java
    Node tos;
    public void push(int x) {
        Node temp;
        if(tos == null) {
            tos=new Node();
            tos.value=x;
            tos.nextNode=null;
        }else {
            temp=new Node();
            temp.value=x;
            temp.nextNode=tos;
            tos=temp;
        }
    }
    public int pop() {
        int value=tos.value;
        tos=tos.nextNode;
        return value;
    }
    public int peek() {
        return tos.value;
    }
    public boolean isStackEmpty() {
        if(tos == null) {
            return true;
        }
        return false;
    }
    public boolean isStackFull() {
        return false;
    }
    public void display() {
        Node temp;
        temp=tos;
        while(temp != null) {
            System.out.println(temp.value);
            temp=temp.nextNode;
        }
    }
}
```

File: TestDynamicStack.java

```java
import java.io.BufferedReader;
import java.io.InputStreamReader;
public class TestDynamicStack {
    public static void main(String[] args) throws Exception{
BufferedReader br=new BufferedReader(new InputStreamReader(System.in));//to read from keyboard
        DynamicStack stack = new DynamicStack();//creating an instance of Stack class
```

```java
boolean wantToExit=false;
do {
    System.out.println();
    System.out.println("[Menu] Press :");
    System.out.println("1 : To push new element into stack.");
    System.out.println("2 : To pop top element from stack.");
    System.out.println("3 : To display peek element.");
    System.out.println("4 : To display all elements of stack.");
    System.out.println("5 : To exit from menu");
    int option=Integer.parseInt(br.readLine());
    switch (option) {
    case 1:
                System.out.println("Enter value to push : ");
                int value = Integer.parseInt(br.readLine());
                stack.push(value);
                break;
    case 2:
        if(stack.isStackEmpty()) {
            System.out.println("You can not pop value: Stack empty");
                break;
            }
            int poppedValue = stack.pop();
            System.out.println("The popped value is : "+poppedValue);
            break;
    case 3:
        if(stack.isStackEmpty()) {
            System.out.println("There is no peek value : Stack empty");
                break;
            }
            int peekValue = stack.peek();
            System.out.println("The peek value is : "+peekValue);
            break;
        case 4:
            if(stack.isStackEmpty()) {
                System.out.println("Stack empty");
                break;
            }
            System.out.println("Values in stack are as follows : ");
            stack.display();
            break;
        case 5:
            System.out.println("Bye");
            wantToExit=true;
            break;
        default:
            System.out.println("Invalid option pressed");
            break;
    }

} while (!wantToExit);
```

```
        }
}
```

Q 4. Implement class **Queue.** The class should implement the following operations:

(i)   void add(int x);
(ii)   int delete();
(iii)   boolean isQueueEmpty()
(iv)   boolean isQueueFull()
(v)   void display()

Write a menu-driven program, which makes use of the Queue class to create the queue of the desired size. The program should prompt the user to select the desired option and then take appropriate action based on the user choice. The user should also be provided the exit option.

Solution
File: Queue.java

```java
public class Queue {
        int s[]=new int[20];
        int front=-1;
        int rear=-1;
        int maxSize;

        public Queue(int n) {
                this.maxSize = n;
        }
        public void add(int x) {
                if(front==-1 && rear==-1) {
                        front = 0;
                }
                rear=(rear+1)%maxSize;
                s[rear]=x;

        }
        public int delete() {
                int value=s[front];
                if(front ==  rear) {
                        front = -1;
                        rear = -1;
                }else {
                        front = (front+1)%maxSize;
                }
                return value;

        }
        public boolean isQueueEmpty() {
                if(front == -1 && rear == -1) {
                        return true;
                }
                return false;

        }
```

```java
    public boolean isQueueFull() {
        int position=(rear+1)%maxSize;
        if(position == front) {
            return true;
        }
        return false;
    }
    public void display() {
        for(int i=front; i != rear; i=(i+1)%maxSize) {
            System.out.println("["+s[i]+"]");
        }
        System.out.println("["+s[rear]+"]");
    }
}
```

File: TestQueus.java

```java
import java.io.BufferedReader;
import java.io.InputStreamReader;

public class TestQueus {
    public static void main(String[] args) throws Exception{
        BufferedReader br=new BufferedReader(new InputStreamReader(System.in));//to read from
keyboard
        System.out.print("Enter the size of Queue (<= 20) : ");
        int sizeOfQueue=Integer.parseInt(br.readLine());
        if (sizeOfQueue > 20) {
            System.out.println("Size of queue must be <= 20");
            return;
        }
        Queue queue = new Queue(sizeOfQueue);//creating an instance of Queue class
        boolean wantToExit=false;
        do {
            System.out.println();
            System.out.println("[Menu] Press :");
            System.out.println("1 : To add new element into queue.");
            System.out.println("2 : To delete one element from queue.");
            System.out.println("3 : To display all elements of queue.");
            System.out.println("4 : To exit from menu");
            int option=Integer.parseInt(br.readLine());
            switch (option) {
                case 1:
                if(queue.isQueueFull()) {
                    System.out.println("You can not add more values: Queue full");
                        break;
                }
                System.out.println("Enter value to add : ");
                int value = Integer.parseInt(br.readLine());
                queue.add(value);
                break;
                case 2:
```

```java
                    if(queue.isQueueEmpty()) {
                        System.out.println("You can not delete value: Queue empty");
                            break;
                    }
                    int dValue = queue.delete();
                    System.out.println("The deleted value is : "+dValue);
                    break;
                case 3:
                    if(queue.isQueueEmpty()) {
                        System.out.println("Queue empty");
                            break;
                    }
                    System.out.println("Values in Queue are as follows : ");
                    queue.display();
                    break;
                case 4:
                    System.out.println("Bye");
                    wantToExit=true;
                    break;
                default:
                    System.out.println("Invalid option pressed");
                    break;
            }
        } while (!wantToExit);
    }
}
```

3 INHERITANCE

Solved Questions

1. Assume that a bank maintains two kinds of accounts for customers, one called as savings account and the other as current account. The savings account provides compound interest and deposit, withdraw facilities. The current account provides no interest. Current account holders should also maintain a minimum balance and if the balance falls below this level, a service charge is imposed.

   Create a class **Account** that stores customer name, account number and type of account. From this drive the classes **CurrAcct** and **SavAcct** to make them more specific. Include necessary methods in order to achieve the following tasks:

   (a) Accept deposit from a customer and update the balance.
   (b) Display the balance
   (c) Compute the deposit interest
   (d) Permit withdrawal and update the balance.
   (e) Check for minimum balance, impose penalty, if necessary, and update the balance.

2. Write class **Employee** which should have constructors and methods as given below:
   public Employee(String name, double salary, int year, int month, int day)
   public String getName()
   public double getSalary()
   public Date getHireDate()
   public void raiseSalary(double byPercent)

   Define class **Manager** by extending class **Employee**. The manager also gets bonus in addition to salary, so the class must have an extra method say **setBonus(double bonus)** to set the bonus. The **getSalary()** method must be overridden in the manager class so as to compute salary as sum of base salary and bonus. This method must make use of the super class method with the same name to get the base salary and then add bonus to it.

   Write a Java program to instantiate objects of classes **Employee** and **Manager** and store them in an array of type **Employee.** The program must finally display the details of each employee.

Unsolved Questions

3. Create the classes in the employee inheritance hierarchy as shown below:

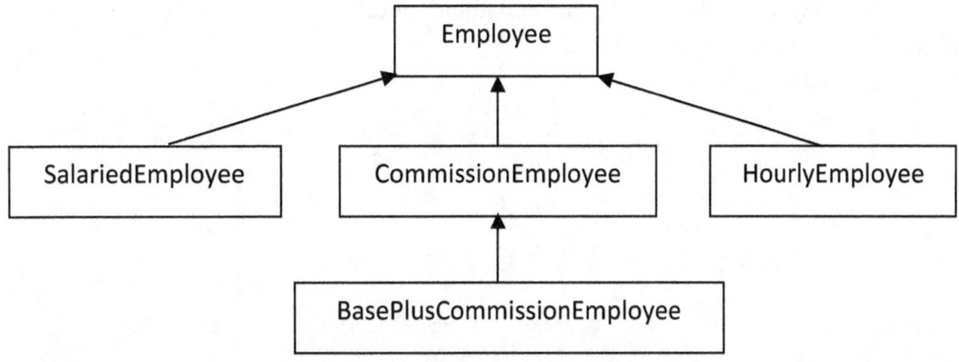

Employee
SalariedEmployee
CommissionEmployee
HourlyEmployee
BasePlusCommissionEmployee

An employee should have a first name, last-name and social-security number. In addition, a **SalariedEmployee** should have a weekly salary; an **HourlyEmployee** should have a wage and a number of hours worked; a **CommissionEmployee** should have a commission rate and gross sales; and a **BasePlusCommissionEmployee** should also have base salary. Each class must have appropriate constructors, set methods and get methods. Also write a program that instantiates objects of each of these classes and outputs all information associated with each object (including inherited information).

4. Write a class **Queue**, which supports the following operations:
    (i)   void add(int x)
    (ii) int delete()

    After writing **Queue** class, write another class **ExtQueue** by sub-classing it and add the following features:

    (i)   void display(); //to display the queue without modifying it
    (ii) boolean isQueueEmpty()
    (iii) boolean isQueueFull()

Solved

Q 1. Assume that a bank maintains two kinds of accounts for customers, one called as savings account and the other as current account. The savings account provides compound interest and deposit, withdraw facilities. The current account provides no interest. Current account holders should also maintain a minimum balance and if the balance falls below this level, a service charge is imposed.

Create a class **Account** that stores customer name, account number and type of account. From this drive the classes **CurrAcct** and **SavAcct** to make them more specific. Include necessary methods in order to achieve the following tasks:

(a) Accept deposit from a customer and update the balance.
(b) Display the balance
(c) Compute the deposit interest
(d) Permit withdrawal and update the balance.
(e) Check for minimum balance, impose penalty, if necessary, and update the balance.

Solution

File: Account.java

```java
public abstract class Account {
    private String accountHolderName;
    private long accountNumber;
    private String accountType; //S for saving, C for current account
    public static final double MINIMUM_BALANCE=1000;
    private double balance;
    public Account(long number, String type, double balance, String name) {
        accountNumber = number;
        accountType = type;
        this.balance = balance;
        accountHolderName = name;
    }
    public long getAccountNumber() {
        return accountNumber;
    }
    public void setAccountNumber(long accountNumber) {
        this.accountNumber = accountNumber;
    }
    public String getAccountType() {
        return accountType;
    }
    public void setAccountType(String accountType) {
        this.accountType = accountType;
    }
    public double getBalance() {
        return balance;
    }
    public void setBalance(double balance) {
```

```java
            this.balance = balance;
        }
        public String getAccountHolderName() {
            return accountHolderName;
        }
        public void setAccountHolderName(String dipositorName) {
            this.accountHolderName = dipositorName;
        }
        public void deposite(double ammount) {
            balance=balance + ammount;
        }
        public abstract boolean withdraw(double ammount);
}
```

File: CurrAcct.java

```java
public class CurrAcct extends Account {
    public static final float SERVICE_CHARGE=25f;
    public CurrAcct(long number, String type, double balance, String name) {
        super(number, type, balance, name);
    }
    @Override
    public boolean withdraw(double ammount) {
        if((getBalance() - ammount) >= Account.MINIMUM_BALANCE) {
            double balance=getBalance() - ammount;
            setBalance(balance);
            return true;
        }else if((getBalance() - ammount) < Account.MINIMUM_BALANCE && (getBalance() -
ammount) >= 0){
            double balance=getBalance() - ammount - CurrAcct.SERVICE_CHARGE;
            setBalance(balance);
            return true;
        }
        return false;
    }
}
```

File: ManageAccounts

```java
import java.io.*;

public class ManageAccounts {
    private static int accountCapacity = 10;
    Account account[]=new Account[ManageAccounts.accountCapacity];
    BufferedReader br=new BufferedReader(new InputStreamReader(System.in));//to read from
keyboard
    private static int lastAccountStatus=-1;
    private static long numberFactor = 198765432101;
    public static void main(String[] args)throws Exception{
        ManageAccounts manageAccount=new ManageAccounts();
        manageAccount.process();
    }
```

```java
private void process() throws Exception {
    boolean wantToExit=false;
    do {
        System.out.println();
        System.out.println("[Menu] Press :");
        System.out.println("1 : To create new account.");
        System.out.println("2 : To view information of account");
        System.out.println("3 : To withdraw money.");
        System.out.println("4 : To deposit money.");
        System.out.println("5 : To exit from menu.");
        System.out.println();
        int option;
        try {
            option=Integer.parseInt(br.readLine());
        } catch (NumberFormatException e) {
            option = -1;
        }
        long accountNumber;
        switch (option) {
            case 1:
                createAccount();
                break;
            case 2:
                System.out.print("Enter account number: ");
                accountNumber=Long.parseLong(br.readLine());
                viewAccountDetailWithInterest(accountNumber);
                break;
            case 3:
                System.out.print("Enter account number: ");
                accountNumber=Long.parseLong(br.readLine());
                withdrawMoney(accountNumber);
                break;
            case 4:
                System.out.print("Enter account number: ");
                accountNumber=Long.parseLong(br.readLine());
                depositeMoney(accountNumber);
                break;
            case 5:
                System.out.println("Bye");
                wantToExit=true;
                break;
            default:
                System.out.println("Invalid option pressed");
                break;
        }

    } while (!wantToExit);
}
private void createAccount() throws Exception {
    if(ManageAccounts.lastAccountStatus == 9) {
```

```java
        System.out.println("Error! Unable to create new account.");
        return;
    }
    System.out.print("Enter customer name: ");
    String name = br.readLine();
    String accountType;
    do {
        System.out.print("Enter account type (S for Saving, C for Current: ");
        accountType = br.readLine();
    } while (!(accountType.equalsIgnoreCase("S") || accountType.equalsIgnoreCase("C")));
    System.out.print("Enter balance (must be >= "+Account.MINIMUM_BALANCE+" Rs.): ");
    double balance;
    balance=Double.parseDouble(br.readLine());
    if(balance < Account.MINIMUM_BALANCE) {
                System.out.print("Error! Minimum Balance must be
                "+Account.MINIMUM_BALANCE+" Rs.): ");
        return;
    }
    ManageAccounts.lastAccountStatus = ManageAccounts.lastAccountStatus + 1;
        long
        accountNumber=ManageAccounts.lastAccountStatus+ManageAccounts.numberFactor
        ;
    if(accountType.equalsIgnoreCase("S")) {
        account[ManageAccounts.lastAccountStatus]=new
SavAcct(accountNumber,accountType,balance,name);
    }else {
        account[ManageAccounts.lastAccountStatus]=new
CurrAcct(accountNumber,accountType,balance,name);
    }
    System.out.println("New account has been created successfully.");
    viewAccountDetail(accountNumber);
}
private void viewAccountDetail(long accountNumber) {
    int accountIndex=(int)(accountNumber-ManageAccounts.numberFactor);
    if(account[accountIndex] != null) {
        System.out.println("Account Detail is as Follows:");
        System.out.println("Name:        "+ account[accountIndex].getAccountHolderName());
        System.out.println("Account number: "+ account[accountIndex].getAccountNumber());
        if(account[accountIndex].getAccountType().equalsIgnoreCase("S")) {
            System.out.println("Account type:    "+ "Saving");
        }else {
            System.out.println("Account type:    "+ "Current");
        }
        System.out.println("Balance:        "+account[accountIndex].getBalance());
    }
    else {
        System.out.println(accountNumber+" account number is not valid");
    }
}
private void viewAccountDetailWithInterest(long accountNumber) {
```

```java
        int accountIndex=(int)(accountNumber-ManageAccounts.numberFactor);
        if(account[accountIndex] != null) {
            System.out.println("Account Detail is as Follows:");
            System.out.println("Name:          "+ account[accountIndex].getAccountHolderName());
            System.out.println("Account number: "+ account[accountIndex].getAccountNumber());
            if(account[accountIndex].getAccountType().equalsIgnoreCase("S")) {
                System.out.println("Account type:   "+ "Saving");
                SavAcct savAcct=((SavAcct)account[accountIndex]);
                double interest = savAcct.calculateInterest();
                savAcct.setBalance(savAcct.getBalance()+interest);
                System.out.println("Interest: "+interest);
            }else {
                System.out.println("Account type:   "+ "Current");

            }
            System.out.println("Balance:        "+account[accountIndex].getBalance());
        }
        else {
            System.out.println(accountNumber+" account number is not valid");
        }
    }
    private void withdrawMoney(long accountNumber) throws Exception {
        int accountIndex=(int)(accountNumber-ManageAccounts.numberFactor);
        if(account[accountIndex] != null) {
            System.out.print("Enter money want to withdraw: ");
            if(account[accountIndex].getAccountType().equalsIgnoreCase("S")) {
                SavAcct savAcct=((SavAcct)account[accountIndex]);
                double interest = savAcct.calculateInterest();
                savAcct.setBalance(savAcct.getBalance()+interest);
                System.out.println("Interest: "+interest);
            }
            double money = Double.parseDouble(br.readLine());
            boolean isSuccess = account[accountIndex].withdraw(money);
            if(isSuccess) {
                System.out.println("Successfull withdraw operation. After Operation: ");
                viewAccountDetail(accountNumber);
            }else {
                System.out.println("Can't perform withdraw operation");
                System.out.println("Minimum balance must be
"+Account.MINIMUM_BALANCE+" Rs.");
                viewAccountDetail(accountNumber);
            }
        }
        else {
            System.out.println(accountNumber+" account number is not valid");
        }
    }
    private void depositeMoney(long accountNumber) throws Exception {
        int accountIndex=(int)(accountNumber-ManageAccounts.numberFactor);
        if(account[accountIndex] != null) {
            System.out.print("Enter money want to diposite: ");
```

```java
            if(account[accountIndex].getAccountType().equalsIgnoreCase("S")) {
                SavAcct savAcct=((SavAcct)account[accountIndex]);
                double interest = savAcct.calculateInterest();
                savAcct.setBalance(savAcct.getBalance()+interest);
                System.out.println("Interest: "+interest);
            }
            double money = Double.parseDouble(br.readLine());
            account[accountIndex].deposite(money);
            System.out.println("Successfull deposit operation. After Operation: ");
            viewAccountDetail(accountNumber);
        }
        else {
            System.out.println(accountNumber+" account number is not valid");
        }
    }
}


File: SavAcct.java
import java.util.*;
public class SavAcct extends Account {
    public static final float interestRate = 0.025f;
    private Date lastInterestDate = null;
    private double interest=0;
    public SavAcct(long number, String type, double balance, String name) {
        super(number, type, balance, name);
        lastInterestDate=new Date();
    }

    @Override
    public boolean withdraw(double ammount) {
        if((getBalance() - ammount) >= Account.MINIMUM_BALANCE) {
            double balance=getBalance() - ammount;
            setBalance(balance);
            return true;
        }
        return false;
    }
    public double calculateInterest() {
        Date currentDate = new Date();
        long diff= currentDate.getTime() - lastInterestDate.getTime();
        Date d2=new Date(diff);
        Calendar cal=Calendar.getInstance();
        cal.setTime(d2);
        int time = cal.get(Calendar.MONTH);
        System.out.println("time: "+time);
        interest = getBalance()*SavAcct.interestRate*time/12; //formula to calculate interest
        lastInterestDate = currentDate;
        return interest;
    }
}
```

Q2. Write class **Employee** which should have constructors and methods as given below:
    public Employee(String name, double salary, int year, int month, int day)
    public String getName()
    public double getSalary()
    public Date getHireDate()
    public void raiseSalary(double byPercent)

Define class **Manager** by extending class **Employee**. The manager also gets bonus in addition to salary, so the class must have an extra method say **setBonus(double bonus)** to set the bonus. The **getSalary()** method must be overridden in the manager class so as to compute salary as sum of base salary and bonus. This method must make use of the super class method with the same name to get the base salary and then add bonus to it.

Write a Java program to instantiate objects of classes **Employee** and **Manager** and store them in an array of type **Employee.** The program must finally display the details of each employee.

Solution
File: Employee.java

```java
package emp;
import java.util.Date;
public class Employee {
    String name;
    double salary;
    java.util.Date hireDate;
    public Employee(String name, Date date, double salary) {
        hireDate = date;
        this.name = name;
        this.salary = salary;
    }
    public java.util.Date getHireDate() {
        return hireDate;
    }
    public void setHireDate(java.util.Date hireDate) {
        this.hireDate = hireDate;
    }
    public String getName() {
        return name;
    }
    public void setName(String name) {
        this.name = name;
    }
    public double getSalary() {
        return salary;
    }
    public void setSalary(double salary) {
```

```java
        this.salary = salary;
    }
    public void raiseSalary(double byPercent) {
        double raiseSalary = salary * byPercent / 100;
        salary = salary + raiseSalary;
    }
}
```

File: Manager.java

```java
package emp;
import java.util.Date;
public class Manager extends Employee {
    private double bonus;
    public Manager(String name, Date date, double salary, double bonus) {
        super(name, date, salary);
        this.bonus = bonus;
    }
    public double getBonus() {
        return bonus;
    }
    public void setBonus(double bonus) {
        this.bonus = bonus;
    }

    public double getSalary() {
        double salary = super.getSalary();
        salary = bonus + salary;
        return salary;
    }
}
```

File: ManageEmployee.java

```java
package emp;
import java.io.*;
import java.util.Date;
public class ManageEmployee {
    private static int capacity = 10;
    Employee employee[]=new Employee[ManageEmployee.capacity];
    BufferedReader br=new BufferedReader(new InputStreamReader(System.in));//to read from keyboard
    private static int lastEmpStatus=-1;
    public static void main(String[] args)throws Exception{
        ManageEmployee manageEmp=new ManageEmployee();
        manageEmp.process();
    }
    private void process() throws Exception {
        boolean wantToExit=false;
        do {
            System.out.println();
            System.out.println("[Menu] Press :");
```

```java
            System.out.println("1 : To register new employee.");
            System.out.println("2 : To view information of employee");
            System.out.println("3 : To raise salary.");
            System.out.println("4 : To set bonus of manager.");
            System.out.println("5 : To view information about all employees.");
            System.out.println("6 : To exit from menu.");
            System.out.println();
            int option;
            try {
                option=Integer.parseInt(br.readLine());
            } catch (NumberFormatException e) {
                option = -1;
            }
            int regId;
            switch (option) {
                case 1:
                    registerEmployee();
                    break;
                case 2:
                    System.out.print("Enter registration id: ");
                    regId=Integer.parseInt(br.readLine());
                    viewEmployeeDetail(regId-1);
                    break;
                case 3:
                    System.out.print("Enter registration id: ");
                    regId=Integer.parseInt(br.readLine());
                    raiseSalary(regId-1);
                    break;
                case 4:
                    System.out.print("Enter registration id: ");
                    regId=Integer.parseInt(br.readLine());
                    setBonus(regId-1);
                    break;
                case 5:
                    for(int i=0; i<=ManageEmployee.lastEmpStatus; i++) {
                        viewEmployeeDetail(i);
                    }
                    break;
                case 6:
                    System.out.println("Bye");
                    wantToExit=true;
                    break;
                default:
                    System.out.println("Invalid option pressed");
                    break;

            }

        } while (!wantToExit);
    }
    private void registerEmployee() throws Exception {
```

```java
        if(ManageEmployee.lastEmpStatus == 9) {
            System.out.println("Error! Unable to create new account.");
            return;
        }
        System.out.print("Enter employee name: ");
        String name = br.readLine();
        System.out.println("Enter designation for employee: (E for Employee or M for Manager)");
        String designation = br.readLine();
        System.out.print("Enter basic salary: ");
        double salary = Double.parseDouble(br.readLine());
        Date hireDate = new Date();//current date
        ManageEmployee.lastEmpStatus = ManageEmployee.lastEmpStatus + 1;
        if(designation.equalsIgnoreCase("E")) {
            employee[ManageEmployee.lastEmpStatus]=new Employee(name,hireDate,salary);
        }else if(designation.equalsIgnoreCase("M")) {
            System.out.print("Enter bonus for manager: ");
            double bonus = Double.parseDouble(br.readLine());
            employee[ManageEmployee.lastEmpStatus]=new
Manager(name,hireDate,salary,bonus);
        }else {
            System.out.print("Error! Designation is not valid");
            return;
        }
        System.out.println("New account has been created successfully.");
        int regId = ManageEmployee.lastEmpStatus;
        System.out.println();
        System.out.println("Your registration id is: "+(regId+1));
        viewEmployeeDetail(regId);
    }
    private void viewEmployeeDetail(int regId) {
        if(employee[regId] != null) {
            System.out.println();
            System.out.println("Employee detail is as Follows:");
            System.out.println("Registration Id: "+(regId+1));
            System.out.println("Name:        "+ employee[regId].getName());
            if(employee[regId] instanceof Manager) {
                System.out.println("Designation: Manager");
                System.out.println("Salary: "+ ((Manager)employee[regId]).getSalary());
            }else {
                System.out.println("Designation: Employee");
                System.out.println("Salary: "+ employee[regId].getSalary());
            }
            System.out.println("Hire Date: "+ employee[regId].getHireDate());
        }
        else {
            System.out.println((regId+1)+" registration id is not valid");
        }
    }
    private void raiseSalary(int regId) throws Exception {
        if(employee[regId] != null) {
```

```java
            System.out.print("Enter the percent by which salary will raise: ");
            double byPercent = Double.parseDouble(br.readLine());
            employee[regId].raiseSalary(byPercent);
            viewEmployeeDetail(regId);
        }
        else {
            System.out.println((regId+1)+" registration id is not valid");
        }
    }
    private void setBonus(int regId) throws Exception {
        if(employee[regId] != null) {
            if(employee[regId] instanceof Manager) {
                Manager manager = (Manager) employee[regId];
                System.out.print("Enter the bonus for manager: ");
                double bonus = Double.parseDouble(br.readLine());
                manager.setBonus(bonus);
                viewEmployeeDetail(regId);
            }else {
                System.out.println((regId+1)+" registration id is not for a Manager");
            }
        }
        else {
            System.out.println((regId+1)+" registration id is not valid");
        }
    }
}
```

4 INTERFACES

1. Define an interface **QueueInt**, with the following method declarations:
   - void add(int x)
   - int delete()

   Write a class **CircularQueue**, which implements the above interface.

2. Extend the interface **QueueInt** defined in the previous question to define a new interface **ExtQueueInt** by adding the following methods:
   - void display(); //to display the queue without modifying it
   - boolean isQueueEmpty()
   - boolean isQueueFull()

3. Define a class, which implements the **ExtQueueInt** interface. You should make use of class **CircularQueue**, which provides the partial implementation of the **ExtQueueInt** interface.

4. Define an interface **Collection** to hold numbers as follows:

```
interface Collection
{       boolean add(int x)
 boolean delete(int x)
 int delete(long index)
 void deleteAll()
 boolean search(int x)
 boolean insert(int x, int index)
 void append(int x)
 void display()
 int get(int index)
}
```

Implement interface **Collection** and derive classes **List**, **SortedList**, **Set**, **SortedSet** and **ArrayList**. The class **List** must provide a linked-list implementation of the **Collection** interface. The class **SortedList** must also provide the linked-list implementation but the elements must remain sorted after each operation. The class **Set** must not allow duplicate elements. The **SortedSet** class should not allow duplicate elements like **Set** class but the elements must be stored in sorted order so as to provide fast search facility. The class **ArrayList** must internally use an array to hold numbers so that elements can be accessed randomly. The internal array must shrink and grow automatically as the number of elements increase and decrease.

Solutions

1. Define an interface **QueueInt**, with the following method declarations:
   - void add(int x)
   - int delete()

   Write a class **CircularQueue**, which implements the above interface.

File: QueueInt.java
```java
public interface QueueInt {
    void add(int x);
    int delete();
}
```

File: CircularQueue.java
```java
public class CircularQueue implements QueueInt {
    int s[]=new int[20];
    int front=-1;
    int rear=-1;
    int maxSize;

    public CircularQueue(int n) {
        this.maxSize = n;
    }
    public void add(int x) {
        if(front==-1 && rear==-1) {
            front = 0;
        }
        rear=(rear+1)%maxSize;
        s[rear]=x;
    }
    public int delete() {
        int value=s[front];
        if(front ==  rear) {
            front = -1;
            rear = -1;
        }else {
            front = (front+1)%maxSize;
        }
        return value;
    }
}
```

2. Extend the interface **QueueInt** defined in the previous question to define a new interface **ExtQueueInt** by adding the following methods:

   - void display(); //to display the queue without modifying it
   - boolean isQueueEmpty()
   - boolean isQueueFull()

Define a class, which implements the **ExtQueueInt** interface. You should make use of class **CircularQueue**, which provides the partial implementation of the **ExtQueueInt** interface.

Solution
File:QueueInt.java

```java
public interface QueueInt {
    void add(int x);
    int delete();
}
```

File: ExtQueueInt.java

```java
interface ExtQueueInt extends QueueInt {
    public boolean isQueueEmpty();
    public boolean isQueueFull();
    public void display();
}
```

File: CircularQueue.java

```java
public class CircularQueue implements QueueInt {
    int s[]=new int[20];
    int front=-1;
    int rear=-1;
    int maxSize;

    public CircularQueue(int n) {
        this.maxSize = n;
    }
    public void add(int x) {
        if(front==-1 && rear==-1) {
            front = 0;
        }
        rear=(rear+1)%maxSize;
        s[rear]=x;
    }
    public int delete() {
        int value=s[front];
        if(front ==  rear) {
            front = -1;
            rear = -1;
        }else {
            front = (front+1)%maxSize;
        }
        return value;
    }
}
```

File: ExtCircularQueue.java

```java
class ExtCircularQueue extends CircularQueue implements ExtQueueInt{
    public ExtCircularQueue(int n) {
        super(n);
```

```java
	}
	public boolean isQueueEmpty() {
		if(front == -1 && rear == -1) {
			return true;
		}
		return false;
	}
	public boolean isQueueFull() {
		int position=(rear+1)%maxSize;
		if(position == front) {
			return true;
		}
		return false;
	}
	public void display() {
		for(int i=front; i != rear; i=(i+1)%maxSize) {
			System.out.println("["+s[i]+"]");
		}
		System.out.println("["+s[rear]+"]");
	}
}
```

5 EXCEPTION HANDLING

Solved Questions

1. Write a method that accepts an array list of integers, an integer, and a subscript as parameters. It should try to put the integer into the array list at the specified subscript, catching the exception IndexOutOfBoundsException, should it be thrown. The method should return true if no exception is thrown and false otherwise.
2. Write a method, Divide, that repeatedly prompts the user at the command line for two integers and computes their quotient as long as the division generates as ArithmeticExcxeption. If no exception occurs, the quotient should be returned.

Unsolved Questions

3. Write a program that repeatedly prompts the user to enter a number at the command line. It stops when a non-numeric value is read and returns the smallest number that was entered.
4. Write a main method that examines its command-line arguments, computes the sum of all of them that are numbers and displays that sum on the command line.
5. Define a class **StackEmptyException** that is a checked exception.
6. Define a class **StackFullException** that defines an unchecked exception.
7. Modify the class **Stack** discussed earlier so as to handle the stackfull and stackempty conditions by throwing **StackEmptyException** and **StackFullException** exceptions respectively. Write a program that makes use of the **Stack** class and handles the above exceptions.
8. Write a program that computes and displays the factorial of a number specified on the command line. It handles all possible user input errors with try/catch.

Solutions

Q1. Write a method that accepts an array list of integers, an integer, and a subscript as parameters. It should try to put the integer into the array list at the specified subscript, catching the exception IndexOutOfBoundsException, should it be thrown. The method should return true if no exception is thrown and false otherwise.

Solution

File: TestArray.java

```java
public class TestArray {

    public static void main(String[] args) {
        int array[] = new int[10];
        int value = 20;
        int index = 2;
        boolean isSuccess = TestArray.put(array,value,index);
        if(isSuccess)
            System.out.println("Success");
        else
            System.out.println("Not Success");
        value = 40;
        index = 10;
        isSuccess = TestArray.put(array,value,index);
        if(isSuccess)
            System.out.println("Success");
        else
            System.out.println("Not Success");
    }

    public static boolean put(int[] array, int value, int index) {
        try {
            array[index] = value;
            return true;
        } catch (IndexOutOfBoundsException e) {
            System.out.println(e);
        }
        return false;
    }
}
```

Q2. Write a method, Divide, that repeatedly prompts the user at the command line for two integers and computes their quotient as long as the division generates as ArithmeticExcxeption. If no exception occurs, the quotient should be returned.

Solution

File: Arithmetic.java

```java
import java.io.*;
import java.awt.image.BufferedImage;
```

```java
class Arithmetic {

  public static void main(String[] args) {
      BufferedReader br = new BufferedReader(new InputStreamReader(System.in));
      do {
          System.out.println();
          System.out.print("Enter first value: ");
          int value1 = 1;
          int value2 = 1;
          try {
              value1 = Integer.parseInt(br.readLine());
          } catch (NumberFormatException e) {
              System.out.print(e);
              continue;
          } catch (IOException e) {
              System.out.print(e);
              continue;
          }
          System.out.println();
          System.out.print("Enter second value: ");
          try {
              value2 = Integer.parseInt(br.readLine());
          } catch (NumberFormatException e) {
              System.out.print(e);
              continue;
          } catch (IOException e) {
              System.out.print(e);
              continue;
          }
          int result = divide(value1,value2);
          System.out.println("Resutlt: "+result);
      } while (true);
  }
  public static int divide(int a, int b) {
      int quotient = a / b;
      return quotient;
  }
}
```

6 STRING CLASS

Solved Questions
1. Write and run a java program that inputs a person's name in the form **First Middle Last** and then prints it in the form **Last First Middle**.
2. Write a program that capitalizes a two-word name. For example, the input **manish bharadwaj** would produce the output **Manish Bhardwaj.**
3. Write a method that accepts a string as a parameter and returns a copy of that same string, but in title case – the first letter of every word is upper case and the other letters in lower case.
4. Write a method that tests whether a string is in title case. First break the string into an array of strings delimited by white space using the split method, then test each substring with the matches method using a regular expression that defines a word in title case.

Unsolved Questions
5. Write a method that accepts a string parameter and returns a copy of that string with all the white spaces removed.
6. Write a method that accepts a string buffer as a parameter and replaces all white space characters with dashes.
7. Write a method that accepts a string, splits the string into substrings, and returns the array of substrings. The delimiters should be any combination of spaces or commas. Use the **StringTokenizer** class to accomplish the subdivision.
8. Read a line of text from the keyboard. Adjust the white space between words so that the whole line is aligned left and right in a line width of 60 characters and print it out.
9. Write a program to convert a given number into words. For example, number 490 should result in the output: four hundred ninety.

Solutions

Q 1. Write and run a java program that inputs a person's name in the form **First Middle Last** and then prints it in the form **Last First Middle**.

Solution:

File: ReverseName.java

```java
class ReverseName {
    public static void main(String[] args) {
        String name = args[2]+" "+args[0]+" "+args[1];
        System.out.println(name);
    }
}
```


Q 2. Write a program that capitalizes a two-word name. For example, the input **manish bharadwaj** would produce the output **Manish Bhardwaj.**

Solution:

File: InitCaps.java

```java
import java.io.*;
public class InitCaps {
    public static void main(String[] args) throws IOException {
        BufferedReader br=new BufferedReader(new InputStreamReader(System.in));
        System.out.println("Enter a name in small case: (for exa.: tn sharma)");
        String name = br.readLine();
            String firstName = name.substring(0,1).toUpperCase() +
            name.substring(1,name.indexOf(" ")).toLowerCase();
            String lastName = name.substring(name.indexOf(" ")+1,name.indexOf("
            ")+2).toUpperCase() + name.substring(name.indexOf(" ")+2).toLowerCase();
        String str = firstName+" "+lastName;
        System.out.println(str);
    }
}
```


Q3. Write a method that accepts a string as a parameter and returns a copy of that same string, but in title case – the first letter of every word is upper case and the other letters in lower case.

Solution:

File: TitleCase.java

```java
import java.io.*;
class TitleCase {
    public static void main(String[] args) throws IOException {
        BufferedReader br=new BufferedReader(new InputStreamReader(System.in));
        System.out.println("Enter a string in small case: ");
```

```java
        StringBuffer orgStr = new StringBuffer(br.readLine());
        TitleCase ic1 = new TitleCase();
        String fmtStr = ic1.initCaps(orgStr);
        System.out.println("Original string : "+orgStr);
        System.out.println("Formatted string: "+fmtStr);
    }
    String initCaps(StringBuffer orgS) {
        String temp = orgS.toString();
        String array[] = temp.split(" ");
        StringBuffer str=new StringBuffer("");
        for (int i = 0; i < array.length; i++) {
                    str.append(array[i].substring(0,1).toUpperCase() +
                    array[i].substring(1).toLowerCase()+" ");
        }
        String str1 = str.toString();
        str1 = str1.substring(0,str.length()-1);
        return str1;
    }
}
```

Q4. Write a method that tests whether a string is in title case. First break the string into an array of strings delimited by white space using the split method, then test each substring with the matches method using a regular expression that defines a word in title case.

Solution:
File:CheckTitleCase.java

```java
import java.io.*;
public class CheckTitleCase{
    public static void main(String[] args) throws IOException {
        BufferedReader br=new BufferedReader(new InputStreamReader(System.in));
        System.out.println("Enter a string (in title case): ");
        String orgStr = br.readLine();
        CheckTitleCase ic1 = new CheckTitleCase();
        boolean isTitleCase = ic1.check(orgStr);
        if(isTitleCase) {
            System.out.println("Given string is in title case");
        }else
            {
            System.out.println("Given string is not in title case");
        }
    }
    boolean check(String orgStr) {
        String fmtStr = initCaps(orgStr);
        return orgStr.matches(fmtStr);
```

```java
    }
String initCaps(String orgS) {
      String array[] = orgS.split(" ");
      String str="";
      for (int i = 0; i < array.length; i++) {
            str = str + array[i].substring(0,1).toUpperCase() +
array[i].substring(1).toLowerCase()+" ";
      }
      str = str.substring(0,str.length()-1);
      return str;
    }
}
```

7 OBJECT AND WRAPPER CLASSES

Solved Questions

1. Make the **LinkedList** class **Cloneable** such that the **clone()** method returns the new linked list using deep cloning i.e. the modification in cloned list must not affect the original list and vice-versa.

2. Write your own wrapper class **Integer**, which can hold data of primitive type **int**. The class **Integer** should also have method to convert the wrapper class object back to primitive. You should also override the **equals()** so that it returns true if the contents of two different **Integer** objects are same. Also override the **hashCode()** methods so that it returns same hashcode for the objects which are treated equal by the **equals()** method.

3. Implement the **LinkedList** class to hold any type of numeric data. Write a program which reads some numbers and stores them in the linked list. Finally compute and display sum of all the numbers stored in the linked list.

4. Write a Java Program that converts the string "7845" to its binary, octal and hexadecimal equivalents.

Unsolved Questions

5. Write a program that converts the characters in the given character array to uppercase letters.

6. Implement the class **Employee** to store information about employee. Override the **toString()** method so that employee's information can be displayed just by displaying employee's object i.e. by passing an employee's object in **println()** method of standard output stream.

7. Implement class HashTable to store key-value pairs. The key must be unique but the value may be duplicate. For example, it can be used to store dictionary entries, where word is a key and its meaning is value. The type of both key and value should be **Object** so that any data type can be stored in hash table. The hash table should provide the following operations:
    (a)   Object put(Object key, Object value)
    (b)   Object get(Object key)
    (c)   Object[] keys()
    (d)   Object[] values()
    (e)   void display()
    (f)   Object delete(Object key)

Solutions

Q1. Make the **LinkedList** class **Cloneable** such that the **clone()** method returns the new linked list using deep cloning i.e. the modification in cloned list must not affect the original list and vice-versa.

```java
class ListNode{
    ListNode nextNode;
    int value;
}

public class LinkedList{
    ListNode start;
    ListNode end;
    int size=0;

    public void add(int x) {
        ListNode temp;
        size++;
        if(end == null) {
            end=new ListNode();
            end.value=x;
            end.nextNode=null;
            start=end;
        }else {
            temp=new ListNode();
            temp.value=x;
            end.nextNode=temp;
            end=temp;
        }
    }
    public int delete(long index) {
        int i=(int)index;
        ListNode temp,prevNode;
        temp=start;
        prevNode = start;
        int value=-1;
        int ind=0;
        while(temp != null) {
            if(ind == i) {
                if(ind == 0) {
                    start=start.nextNode;
                    break;
                }
                value=temp.value;
                prevNode.nextNode=temp.nextNode;
                break;
            }
            prevNode = temp;
```

```java
                temp=temp.nextNode;
                ind++;
            }
            size--;
            return value;
        }
    public boolean delete(int x) {
        ListNode temp,prevNode;
        temp=start;
        prevNode = start;
        size--;
        while(temp != null) {
            if(temp.value == x) {
                prevNode.nextNode=temp.nextNode;
                return true;
            }
            prevNode = temp;
            temp=temp.nextNode;
        }
        return false;
    }
    public void deleteAll() {
        start = null;
        end = null;
        size=0;
    }

    public boolean search(int x) {
        ListNode temp;
        temp=start;
        while(temp != null) {
            if(temp.value == x) {
                return true;
            }
            temp=temp.nextNode;
        }
        return false;
    }
    public void insert(int x, int index) {
        size++;
        ListNode temp,prevNode;
        temp=start;
        prevNode = start;
        int ind=0;
        while(temp != null) {
            if(ind == index) {
                ListNode newNode=new ListNode();
                newNode.value=x;
                if(ind == 0) {
                    newNode.nextNode = temp;
```

```java
            }else {
                    prevNode.nextNode=newNode;
                    newNode.nextNode=temp;
            }
            break;
        }
        prevNode = temp;
        temp=temp.nextNode;
        ind++;
    }
}
public LinkedList sort() {
    int temp=-1;
    ListNode tempNode = start;
    while(tempNode != null) {
        ListNode prevNode = start;
        ListNode nextNode = prevNode.nextNode;
        while(nextNode != null) {
            if(prevNode.value > nextNode.value) {
                    temp = prevNode.value;
                    prevNode.value = nextNode.value;
                    nextNode.value = temp;
            }
            prevNode = prevNode.nextNode;
            nextNode = prevNode.nextNode;
        }
        tempNode=tempNode.nextNode;
    }
    return LinkedList.this;
}
public int get(int index) {
    ListNode temp;
    temp=start;
    int ind=0;
    int value=-1;
    while(temp != null) {
        if(ind == index) {
            value = temp.value;
            break;
        }
        temp=temp.nextNode;
        ind++;
    }
    return value;
}
public void display() {
    StringBuffer sb=new StringBuffer("[");
    ListNode temp;
    temp=start;
    while(temp != null) {
```

```java
            sb.append(temp.value+", ");
            temp=temp.nextNode;
        }
            String strList=sb.toString().substring(0,sb.toString().lastIndexOf(", "))+"]";
        System.out.println(strList);
    }
    public Object clone() {
        LinkedList list = new LinkedList();
        ListNode start;
        ListNode end;
        int size = this.size;
        ListNode temp1=new ListNode();
        start = temp1;
        ListNode temp=this.start;
        ListNode pretemp = null;
        while(temp != null) {
            temp1.value = temp.value;
            pretemp = temp1;
            ListNode ln = new ListNode();
            temp1.nextNode = ln;
            temp1 = ln;
            temp=temp.nextNode;
        }
        pretemp.nextNode = null;
        list.start = start;
        list.end = pretemp;
        list.size = size;
        return list;
    }
}

public class TestLinkedList {
    public static void main(String[] args) {
        LinkedList list=new LinkedList();
        list.add(10);
        list.add(20);
        list.add(17);
        list.add(5);
        list.add(10);
        list.display();
        System.out.println(list.get(3));
        list.insert(100,3);
        list.display();
        list.delete(100);
        list.display();
        list.delete(0l);
        list.display();
        list.delete(3l);
        list.display();
        list.delete(2l);
```

```
                list.display();
                LinkedList list1=(LinkedList)list.clone();
                System.out.println("Cloned List: ");
                list1.display();
                list1.insert(117,1);
                list1.add(10);
                list1.add(20);
                list1.add(17);
                list1.add(5);
                list1.add(10);
                System.out.println("Cloned List: ");
                list1.display();
                System.out.println("Original List: ");
                list.display();

        }

}
```

Q.2. Write your own wrapper class **Integer**, which can hold data of primitive type **int**. The class **Integer** should also have method to convert the wrapper class object back to primitive. You should also override the **equals()** so that it returns true if the contents of two different **Integer** objects are same. Also override the **hashCode()** methods so that it returns same hashcode for the objects which are treated equal by the **equals()** method.

Solution

```
public class Integer {
    private int value;
    public Integer(int value) {
        this.value = value;
    }
    int intValue() {
        return value;
    }
//  Override
    public boolean equals(Object obj) {
        if(value == ((Integer)obj).value) {
            return true;
        }
        return false;
    }
//  Override
    public int hashCode() {
        return value * 555 % 9999;
    }
//  Override
    public String toString() {
        return String.valueOf(value);
    }
```

```java
}
class TestInteger {
    public static void main(String[] args) {
        Integer integer = new Integer(44);
        Integer integer1 = new Integer(45);
        System.out.println(integer);
        System.out.println(integer1);
        System.out.println(integer.equals(integer1));
            System.out.println("Hash code of first obj: "+integer.hashCode());
            System.out.println("Hash code of second obj: "+integer1.hashCode());
        integer = new Integer(44);
        integer1 = new Integer(44);
        System.out.println(integer);
        System.out.println(integer1);
        System.out.println(integer.equals(integer1));
            System.out.println("Hash code of first obj: "+integer.hashCode());
            System.out.println("Hash code of second obj: "+integer1.hashCode());
    }
}
```

Q 3.Implement the **LinkedList** class to hold any type of numeric data. Write a program which reads some numbers and stores them in the linked list. Finally compute and display sum of all the numbers stored in the linked list.

Solution

```java
package util;

class ListNode{
    ListNode nextNode;
    Number value;
}
public class LinkedList{
    ListNode start;
    ListNode end;
    int size=0;
    public void add(Number x) {
        ListNode temp;
        size++;
        if(end == null) {
            end=new ListNode();
            end.value=x;
            end.nextNode=null;
            start=end;
        }else {
            temp=new ListNode();
            temp.value=x;
            end.nextNode=temp;
            end=temp;
```

```java
        }
    }
    public Number delete(long index) {
        int i=(int)index;
        ListNode temp,prevNode;
        temp=start;
        prevNode = start;
        Number value=null;
        int ind=0;
        while(temp != null) {
            if(ind == i) {
                if(ind == 0) {
                    start=start.nextNode;
                    break;
                }
                value=temp.value;
                prevNode.nextNode=temp.nextNode;
                break;
            }
            prevNode = temp;
            temp=temp.nextNode;
            ind++;
        }
        size--;
        return value;
    }
    public boolean delete(Number x) {
        ListNode temp,prevNode;
        temp=start;
        prevNode = start;
        size--;
        while(temp != null) {
            if(temp.value.byteValue() == x.byteValue()) {
                prevNode.nextNode=temp.nextNode;
                return true;
            }
            prevNode = temp;
            temp=temp.nextNode;
        }
        return false;
    }
    public void deleteAll() {
        start = null;
        end = null;
        size=0;
    }

    public boolean search(Number x) {
        ListNode temp;
        temp=start;
```

```java
        while(temp != null) {
            if(temp.value.byteValue() == x.byteValue()) {
                return true;
            }
            temp=temp.nextNode;
        }
        return false;
    }
    public void insert(Number x, int index) {
        size++;
        ListNode temp,prevNode;
        temp=start;
        prevNode = start;
        int ind=0;
        while(temp != null) {
            if(ind == index) {
                ListNode newNode=new ListNode();
                newNode.value=x;
                if(ind == 0) {
                    newNode.nextNode = temp;
                }else {
                    prevNode.nextNode=newNode;
                    newNode.nextNode=temp;
                }
                break;
            }
            prevNode = temp;
            temp=temp.nextNode;
            ind++;
        }
    }
    public Number get(int index) {
        ListNode temp;
        temp=start;
        int ind=0;
        Number value=null;
        while(temp != null) {
            if(ind == index) {
                value = temp.value;
                break;
            }
            temp = temp.nextNode;
            ind++;
        }
        return value;
    }
    public void display() {
        StringBuffer sb=new StringBuffer("[");
        ListNode temp;
        temp=start;
```

```java
        while(temp != null) {
            sb.append(temp.value+", ");
            temp=temp.nextNode;
        }
            String strList=sb.toString().substring(0,sb.toString().lastIndexOf(", "))+"]";
        System.out.println(strList);
    }
}


package util;
public class TestLinkedList {
    public static void main(String[] args) {
        double sum=0;
        LinkedList list=new LinkedList();
        list.add(new Double(10));
        list.add(new Double(20));
        list.add(new Double(17));
        list.add(new Double(5));
        list.add(new Double(10));
        list.display();
        System.out.println(list.get(3));
        list.insert(new Double(100),3);
        list.display();
        list.delete(new Double(100));
        list.display();
        for (int i = 0; i < list.size; i++) {
            sum += (Double)list.get(i);
        }
        System.out.println("Sum: "+sum);
        System.out.println();
        double sum1=0;
        LinkedList list1=new LinkedList();
        list1.add(new Integer(10));
        list1.add(new Integer(20));
        list1.add(new Integer(17));
        list1.add(new Integer(5));
        list1.add(new Integer(10));
        list1.display();
        System.out.println(list.get(3));
        list1.insert(new Integer(100),3);
        list1.display();
        list1.delete(new Integer(100));
        list1.display();
        for (int i = 0; i < list.size; i++) {
            sum1 += (Integer)list1.get(i);
        }
        System.out.println("Sum: "+sum1);
    }
}
```

Q4. Write a Java Program that converts the string "7845" to its binary, octal and hexadecimal equivalents.

Solution

```java
class NumberConvert {
    public static void main(String[] args) {
        String str = "7845";
        Long value = Long.parseLong(str);
            System.out.println("Binary String: "+Long.toBinaryString(value));
            System.out.println("Octal String: "+Long.toOctalString(value));
            System.out.println("Hexadecimal String: "+Long.toHexString(value));
    }

}
```

8 MULTITHREADING

Solved Questions

1. Write a program that displays the name of the thread that executes main.
2. Write a Java program to demonstrate that as a high-priority thread executes, it will delay the execution of all lower priority threads.
3. If your system supports time-slicing, write a java program that demonstrates time-slicing among several equal-priority threads. Also show that a lower priority thread's execution is deferred by the time-slicing of higher priority threads.
4. Write a java program that demonstrates a high priority thread using **sleep** to give lower priority threads a chance to run.
5. Write a java program that reads numbers from keyboard in two arrays say **a** and **b**. The program should create one thread for sorting each array. The main thread should block till both the treads complete sorting and then merge the two sorted arrays and finally should display merged array on the output stream.
   Hint: Make use of **join()** method to block the main thread till both the sort threads complete.

Unsolved Questions

6. Solve the previous problem by using **isAlive()** method instead of **join()** method.
7. Write a class whose objects hold a current value and have a method that will add to the value. Write a program that creates such an object, creates multiple threads, and invokes the adding method repeatedly from each thread. Write the class so that no addition can be lost.
8. Modify the previous problem to use static data and methods.
9. Write a java program which creates instance of **Stack** class and creates two threads to concurrently access the same stack. Demonstrate that the concurrent operations may lead to inconsistency. Modify the **Stack** class to ensure that the concurrent operations do not lead to inconsistency.
10. A bank account is operated by a father and his son. The account is opened with an initial deposit of Rs. 1000. The father and son can access the account concurrently. Create two threads for performing transactions on the bank account one for father and one for son. Demonstrate that the concurrent operations may lead to inconsistency. Then make appropriate modifications to ensure that the concurrent operations do not lead to inconsistency.

Solutions

Q1. Write a program that displays the name of the thread that executes main.

Solution
```java
class First{
    public static void main(String[] args) {
        Thread currentThread = Thread.currentThread();
        System.out.println("Name: "+currentThread.getName());
            System.out.println("Group: "+currentThread.getThreadGroup());
            System.out.println("Priority: "+currentThread.getPriority());
        System.out.println("State: "+currentThread.getState());

    }
}
```

Q2.Write a Java program to demonstrate that as a high-priority thread executes, it will delay the execution of all lower priority threads.

Solution
```java
class PriorityBasedExample implements Runnable{
    public PriorityBasedExample() {
        Thread t1 = new Thread(this,"First");
        t1.setPriority(Thread.MAX_PRIORITY);
        Thread t2 = new Thread(this,"Second");
        t2.setPriority(Thread.MIN_PRIORITY);
        Thread t3 = new Thread(this,"Third");
        t3.setPriority(Thread.NORM_PRIORITY);
        t2.start();
        t3.start();
        t1.start();
    }
    public static void main(String[] args) {
        PriorityBasedExample pbe=new PriorityBasedExample();
    }
    public void run() {
        Thread thread = Thread.currentThread();
        for(int i=1; i< 4; i++) {
            System.out.println(thread.getName()+" "+thread.getPriority());
        }
    }
}
```

Q3 If your system supports time-slicing, write a java program that demonstrates time-slicing among several equal-priority threads. Also show that a lower priority thread's execution is deferred by the time-slicing of higher priority threads.

Solution
```java
public class TimeSlicing implements Runnable{
```

```java
        int value = 0;
        boolean stopFalg = false;
        public TimeSlicing() {
            Thread t1 = new Thread(this,"First");
            t1.setPriority(Thread.MAX_PRIORITY);
            Thread t2 = new Thread(this,"Second");
            t2.setPriority(Thread.MIN_PRIORITY);
            Thread t3 = new Thread(this,"Third");
            t3.setPriority(Thread.NORM_PRIORITY);
            Thread t4 = new Thread(this,"Forth");
            t4.setPriority(Thread.NORM_PRIORITY);
            Thread t5 = new Thread(this,"Fifth");
            t5.setPriority(Thread.NORM_PRIORITY);
            t1.start();
            t2.start();
            t3.start();
            t4.start();
            t5.start();
            try {
                Thread.sleep(200);
            } catch (InterruptedException e) {
                System.out.println(e);
            }
            stopFalg = true;

        }
        public static void main(String[] args) {
            TimeSlicing pbe=new TimeSlicing();
        }
          public void run() {
            Thread thread = Thread.currentThread();
            while(!stopFalg) {
                value++;
                System.out.println(thread.getName()+" "+value);
            }
        }
    }
}
```

Q4. Write a java program that demonstrates a high priority thread using **sleep** to give lower priority threads a chance to run.

```java
class NewThread extends Thread{

    NewThread() {
        super();
        start();
    }

    NewThread(String name) {
        super(name);
        start();
```

```java
        }
//      Override
        public void run() {
            Thread thread = Thread.currentThread();
            for(int i=1; i< 4; i++) {
                        System.out.println(thread.getName()+" "+thread.getPriority());
                try {
                    sleep(200);
                } catch (InterruptedException e) {
                    System.out.println(e);
                }
            }
        }
}
class SleepExample {
    public static void main(String[] args) {
        NewThread t1 = new NewThread("First");
        t1.setPriority(Thread.MAX_PRIORITY);
        NewThread t2 = new NewThread("Second");
        t2.setPriority(Thread.MIN_PRIORITY);
        NewThread t3 = new NewThread("Third");
        t3.setPriority(Thread.NORM_PRIORITY);
    }
}
```

Q5. Write a java program that reads numbers from keyboard in two arrays say **a** and **b**. The program should create one thread for sorting each array. The main thread should block till both the treads complete sorting and then merge the two sorted arrays and finally should display merged array on the output stream.

Hint: Make use of **join()** method to block the main thread till both the sort threads complete.

Solution

```java
public class Sort implements Runnable {
    private int array[];
    public Sort(int[] array) {
        this.array = array;
    }

    public void run() {
        for(int i=0;i<array.length;i++) {
            for (int j = 0; j < array.length-1; j++) {
                if(array[j] > array[j+1]) {
                    int temp = array[j];
                    array[j] = array[j+1];
                    array[j+1] = temp;
                }
            }
        }
    }
}
```

```java
import java.io.*;
class TestSort {
    int a[] = new int[5];
    int b[] = new int[4];
    public static void main(String[] args) {
            BufferedReader br = new BufferedReader(new InputStreamReader(System.in));
        System.out.println("Enter ineger values for first array: ");
        TestSort ts = new TestSort();
        for(int i=0; i < ts.a.length; i++) {
            try {
                ts.a[i] = Integer.parseInt(br.readLine());
            } catch (NumberFormatException e) {
                System.out.println(e);
                ts.a[i] = 0;
            } catch (IOException e) {
                System.out.println(e);
                ts.a[i] = 0;
            }
        }
        System.out.println("Enter ineger values for second array: ");
        for(int i=0; i < ts.b.length; i++) {
            try {
                ts.b[i] = Integer.parseInt(br.readLine());
            } catch (NumberFormatException e) {
                System.out.println(e);
                ts.a[i] = 0;
            } catch (IOException e) {
                System.out.println(e);
                ts.a[i] = 0;
            }
        }
        Thread t1 = new Thread(new Sort(ts.a));
        Thread t2 = new Thread(new Sort(ts.b));
        t1.start();
        t2.start();
        try {
            t1.join();
            t2.join();
        } catch (InterruptedException e) {
            System.out.println(e);
        }
        System.out.println("After Sorting");
        System.out.println("Array a: ");
        System.out.print("{");
        for (int i = 0; i < ts.a.length; i++) {
            System.out.print(ts.a[i]);
            if(i != ts.a.length-1) {
                System.out.print(", ");
            }
```

```java
        }
        System.out.println("}");
        System.out.println("Array b: ");
        System.out.print("{");
        for (int i = 0; i < ts.b.length; i++) {
            System.out.print(ts.b[i]);
            if(i != ts.b.length-1) {
                System.out.print(", ");
            }
        }
        System.out.println("}");
        int mergedArray[] = mergeArrays(ts.a,ts.b);
        System.out.println("Merged Array: ");
        System.out.print("{");
        for (int i = 0; i < mergedArray.length; i++) {
            System.out.print(mergedArray[i]);
            if(i != mergedArray.length-1) {
                System.out.print(", ");
            }
        }
        System.out.println("}");
        //to sort merged array
        Thread tm = new Thread(new Sort(mergedArray));
        tm.start();
        try {
            tm.join();
        } catch (InterruptedException e) {
            System.out.println(e);
        }
        System.out.println("After sorting merged array: ");
        System.out.print("{");
        for (int i = 0; i < mergedArray.length; i++) {
            System.out.print(mergedArray[i]);
            if(i != mergedArray.length-1) {
                System.out.print(", ");
            }
        }
        System.out.println("}");

    }
    private static int[] mergeArrays(int[] a, int[] b) {

        int length = (a.length+b.length);
        int mergedArray[] = new int[length];
        int j = 0;
        for(int i=0;i<mergedArray.length;i++) {
            if(i < a.length) {
                mergedArray[i] = a[i];
            }else {
                mergedArray[i] = b[j];
```

```
                j++;
            }
        }
    return mergedArray;
    }
}
```

9 Collection and map classes

Solved Questions

1. Write a program to count the number of occurrences of each word in a given string.

2. Modify the above program to count the number of occurrences of each letter rather than of each word.

3. Write a method that tests whether a string is in title case. First break the string into an array of strings delimited by white space using the split method, then test each substring with the matches method using a regular expression that defines a word in title case.

4. Write a program that reads in a series of first names and stores them in a LinkedList. Do not store duplicate names. Allow the user to search for a first name.

5. Write a program which reads names and marks of students from the keyboard and stores them in a hash table. The program then displays the name and marks on the monitor. The user then gets choices for adding more entries, updating existing entries, deleting wrong entries and for exiting after displaying final list and storing final list in a file.

Unsolved Questions

6. A properties file contains pairs of person name and phone numbers. It is assumed that person name is unique and acts as a key. Write a java program to read the contents of the file in a **Properties** object. The program then provides a menu of choices to the user to perform following operations:
   (a)   Adding a new entry
   (b)   Deleting an existing entry
   (c)   Updating an existing entry
   (d)   Searching
   (e)   Updating the properties file so as to reflect the current   status, and
   (f)   Exiting

7. Write a program which reads student's records from keyboard. Each record consists of roll no, name and marks in 3 subjects. Store the records in an object of class **TreeMap**. The roll no. should be used as a key and value should be an object containing student's details. The students' records should be added such that they remain sorted on total marks. Finally display the students' records.

8. Write a program to read key-value pairs of words and their meanings from a properties file and store in a properties table. The program then should prompts the user to enter a word and should either display the word's meaning or a message indicating that word is not present in the dictionary.

9. Write a program that determines and prints the number of duplicate words in a sentence. Treat uppercase and lowercase letters the same.

10. Write a program that uses a StringTokenizer to tokenize a line of text input by the user and places each token in a sorted tree. Print the elements of the sorted tree.

Solved

Q1. Write a program to count the number of occurrences of each word in a given string.

Solution

```java
import java.io.*;
import java.util.*;

public class CountDuplicates {
    public static void main(String[] args) {
        CountDuplicates app = new CountDuplicates();
        BufferedReader br = new BufferedReader(new InputStreamReader(System.in));
        System.out.println("Enter any string: ");
        String str;
        try {
            str = br.readLine();
            int duplicates = app.count(str);
            System.out.println("Number of duplicates: "+duplicates);
        } catch (IOException e) {
            System.out.println(e);
        }
    }
    int count(String str){
        Hashtable<String,Integer> table = new Hashtable<String,Integer>();
        StringTokenizer st = new StringTokenizer(str,", :\"\n\t':");
        while(st.hasMoreTokens()) {
            String key = st.nextToken().toLowerCase();
            if(table.containsKey(key)) {
                int value = table.get(key)+1;
                table.put(key,value);
            }else {
                int value = 1;
                table.put(key,value);
            }
        }
        int count = 0;
        Enumeration enumeration = table.keys();
        while(enumeration.hasMoreElements()) {
            String key = (String)enumeration.nextElement();
            int value = table.get(key);
            if(value > 1) {
                count++;
            }
        }
        return count;
    }
}
```

Q2. Modify the above program to count the number of occurrences of each letter rather than of each word.

Solution

```java
import java.io.*;
import java.util.*;

public class CountLetters {
    public static void main(String[] args) {
        CountLetters app = new CountLetters();
        BufferedReader br = new BufferedReader(new InputStreamReader(System.in));
        System.out.println("Enter any string: ");
        String str;
        try {
            str = br.readLine();
            app.count(str);
        } catch (IOException e) {
            System.out.println(e);
        }
    }
    void count(String str){
        Hashtable<Character,Integer> table = new Hashtable<Character,Integer>();
        char ch[] = str.toCharArray();
        for(int i=0;i<ch.length;i++) {
            if(table.containsKey(ch[i])) {
                int value = table.get(ch[i])+1;
                table.put(ch[i],value);
            }else {
                int value = 1;
                table.put(ch[i],value);
            }
        }
        System.out.println("Letter\t\tOccurrance");
        Enumeration enumeration = table.keys();
        while(enumeration.hasMoreElements()) {
            char key = (Character)enumeration.nextElement();
            System.out.println(key+"\t\t"+table.get(key));
        }
    }
}
```

Q3. Write a method that tests whether a string is in title case. First break the string into an array of strings delimited by white space using the split method, then test each substring with the matches method using a regular expression that defines a word in title case.

Solution

```java
import java.io.*;
import java.util.*;
```

```java
public class FifthExample {
    public static void main(String[] args) {
        FifthExample app = new FifthExample();
        BufferedReader br = new BufferedReader(new InputStreamReader(System.in));
        System.out.println("Enter any string: ");
        String str;
        try {
            str = br.readLine();
            app.insert(str);
        } catch (IOException e) {
            System.out.println(e);
        }
    }
    void insert(String str){
        TreeSet<String> tree = new TreeSet<String>();
        StringTokenizer st = new StringTokenizer(str,", :\"\n\t':");
        while(st.hasMoreTokens()) {
            String value = st.nextToken();
            tree.add(value);
        }

        Iterator<String> iterator = tree.iterator();
        while(iterator.hasNext()) {
            String value = iterator.next();
            System.out.println(value);
        }
    }
}
```

Q4. Write a program that reads in a series of first names and stores them in a LinkedList. Do not store duplicate names. Allow the user to search for a first name.

Solution

```java
import java.io.*;
import java.util.LinkedList;

public class First {
    LinkedList<String> linkedList;
    BufferedReader br;
    public First() {
        linkedList = new LinkedList<String>();
        br = new BufferedReader(new InputStreamReader(System.in));
        try {
            process();
        } catch (IOException e) {
            System.out.println(e);
        }
    }
    public static void main(String[] args) throws IOException {
```

```java
        First app = new First();
    }
private void process() throws IOException {
    boolean wantToExit=false;
    do {
            System.out.println();
            System.out.println("[Menu] Press :");
            System.out.println("1 : To add new names.");
            System.out.println("2 : To search name");
            System.out.println("3 : To exit from menu.");
            System.out.println();
            int option;
            try {
                option=Integer.parseInt(br.readLine());
            } catch (NumberFormatException e) {
                option = -1;
            }
            switch (option) {
                case 1:
                    store();
                    break;
                case 2:
                    System.out.print("Enter first name: ");
                    String name=br.readLine();
                    int index = search(name);
                    if(index == -1) {
                        System.out.println("Name not exist in list");
                    }else {
                        System.out.println("Name exists at index: "+index);
                    }
                    break;
                case 3:
                    System.out.println("Bye");
                    wantToExit=true;
                    break;
                default:
                    System.out.println("Invalid option pressed");
                    break;
            }

    } while (!wantToExit);
}
void store(){
    System.out.println("Enter first names (or 'stop'):");
    String str;
    try {
        do {
            str = br.readLine();
            if(!checkDuplicate(str)) {
                linkedList.add(str);
```

```
            }
        }while(!str.equalsIgnoreCase("stop"));
    } catch (IOException e) {
        System.out.println(e);
    }
}
boolean checkDuplicate(String name) {
    return linkedList.contains(name);
}
int search(String name) {
    return linkedList.indexOf(name);
}
}
```

Q5. Write a program which reads names and marks of students from the keyboard and stores them in a hash table. The program then displays the name and marks on the monitor. The user then gets choices for adding more entries, updating existing entries, deleting wrong entries and for exiting after displaying final list and storing final list in a file.

Solution

```java
import java.io.*;
import java.util.*;

public class ManageStudentRecord {
    protected BufferedReader br;
    protected Hashtable<String, Integer> table;
    public ManageStudentRecord() {
        br=new BufferedReader(new InputStreamReader(System.in));//to read from keyboard
        table = new Hashtable<String, Integer>();
    }
    public static void main(String[] args)throws Exception{
        ManageStudentRecord manageRecord=new ManageStudentRecord();
        manageRecord.newStudentRecord();
        manageRecord.viewAllStudentDetail();
        manageRecord.process();
    }
    protected void process() throws Exception {
        boolean wantToExit=false;
        do {
            System.out.println();
            System.out.println("[Menu] Press :");
            System.out.println("1 : To enter new student records.");
            System.out.println("2 : To view information of a student.");
            System.out.println("3 : To view information about all students.");
            System.out.println("4 : To update information of a student.");
            System.out.println("5 : To delete information of a student.");
            System.out.println("6 : To store final list into file.");
            System.out.println("7 : To exit from menu.");
            System.out.println();
```

```java
            int option;
            try {
                option=Integer.parseInt(br.readLine());
            } catch (NumberFormatException e) {
                option = -1;
            }
            String name;
            switch (option) {
                case 1:
                    newStudentRecord();
                    break;
                case 2:
                    System.out.print("Enter student name: ");
                    name=br.readLine();
                    viewStudentDetail(name);
                    break;
                case 3:
                    viewAllStudentDetail();
                    break;
                case 4:
                    System.out.print("Enter student name: ");
                    name=br.readLine();
                    updateStudentDetail(name);
                    break;
                case 5:
                    System.out.print("Enter student name: ");
                    name=br.readLine();
                    deleteWrongEntry(name);
                    break;
                case 6:
                    System.out.print("Enter file name: ");
                    String fileName=br.readLine();
                    saveToFile(fileName);
                    break;
                case 7:
                    System.out.println("Bye");
                    wantToExit=true;
                    break;
                default:
                    System.out.println("Invalid option pressed");
                    break;
            }

        } while (!wantToExit);
    }
    private void saveToFile(String fileName) {
        PrintWriter out = null;
        try {
            out = new PrintWriter(new FileWriter(fileName));
            Enumeration enumeration = table.keys();
```

```java
            while(enumeration.hasMoreElements()) {
                String key = (String)enumeration.nextElement();
                String entry = key+"="+table.get(key);
                out.println(entry);
            }
            System.out.println("Final list has saved successfully in file: "+fileName);
        } catch (IOException e) {
            System.out.println(e);
        }finally {
            if(out != null) {
                out.close();
            }
        }
    }
}
    private void deleteWrongEntry(String name) {
        table.remove(name);
        System.out.println("Entry of student "+name+" has been deleted successfully");
    }
    private void updateStudentDetail(String name) {
        System.out.println("Enter the marks for of "+name);
        int marks;
        try {
            marks = Integer.parseInt(br.readLine());
            table.put(name,marks);
            System.out.println("Entry of student "+name+" has updated successfully");
            viewStudentDetail(name);
        } catch (NumberFormatException e) {
            System.out.println(e);
        } catch (IOException e) {
            System.out.println(e);
        }
    }
    protected void newStudentRecord(){
        boolean stopFlag = false;
        try {
            do {
                System.out.println("Enter sudent name: ");
                String name = br.readLine();
                System.out.println("Enter marks: ");
                int marks = Integer.parseInt(br.readLine());
                table.put(name,marks);
                System.out.println("Are you want to 'stop'(Y/N): ");
                String res = br.readLine();
                if(res.equalsIgnoreCase("y")) {
                    stopFlag = true;
                }
            } while (!stopFlag);
        } catch (NumberFormatException e) {
            System.out.println(e);
        } catch (IOException e) {
```

```java
            System.out.println(e);
        }
    }
    protected void viewStudentDetail(String name) {
        System.out.println("Name:        "+name);
        System.out.println("Marks:       "+table.get(name));
    }
    protected void viewAllStudentDetail() {
        System.out.println("All entries are as follows: ");
        Enumeration enumeration = table.keys();
        while(enumeration.hasMoreElements()) {
            String key = (String)enumeration.nextElement();
            System.out.println(key+":\t\t"+table.get(key));
        }
    }
}


}
```

10 INPUT/OUTPUT

Solved Questions

1. Write a Java Program that finds the largest file in the given directory.
2. Write a Java Program that lists the file name, its size and the last modified date for all the files in the specified directory just like the **dir** command of DOS.
3. Write a program that accepts names of input & output text files as command-line arguments, and copies the input file to the output file, converting all letters to the uppercase. The input file should be read using **BufferedReader** stream and contents to output file should be written using **PrintWriter** stream.
4. Write a program to input the Name, Sex, Height and Weight of n persons from the keyboard and store them in a file "height.dat".

Unsolved Questions

5. Write a java program to read the file "height.dat" created in the above program and display on the monitor.
6. Modify the above program so as to display the output sorted in ascending order of names.
7. A set of double values are stored in two different files file1.dat and file2.dat. Write a java program to read these files and find the average of the values.
8. A list containing the following details is given:

    Name   :   String
    Marks1   :   int
    Marks2   :   int
    Marks3   :   int

    Write a class to describe the above fields. Create objects for 5 sets of values and store the data in a file **"result.dat"** using **ObjectOutputStream** class.
9. Read the file **"result.dat"** created in the above program and display the data.
10. Write a program to count the number of characters, words and lines in a given file. The file name is to be given through the command line argument.

Solutions

Q1. Write a Java Program that finds the largest file in the given directory.

Solution

```java
import java.io.File;
import java.util.ResourceBundle;
public class FindLargestFile {
    String fileName = null;
    double fileSize = 0;

    public FindLargestFile(File file) {
        getAllFiles(file);
    }
    public static void main(String[] args) {
        String dir = args[0];
        File file = null;
        try {
            file = new File(dir);
        } catch (RuntimeException e) {
            System.out.println(e);
        }
        System.out.println("Searching...");
        FindLargestFile flf = new FindLargestFile(file);
        System.out.println("Largest file name: "+flf.fileName);
        System.out.println("file size: "+flf.fileSize);
    }
    void getAllFiles(File dir) {
        if(dir.isDirectory()) {
            File[] files = dir.listFiles();
            for(int i=0; i< files.length; i++) {
                getAllFiles(files[i]);
            }
        }else {
            if(fileSize < dir.length()) {
                fileSize = dir.length();
                fileName = dir.getName();
            }
        }
    }
}
```

Q2. Write a Java Program that lists the file name, its size and the last modified date for all the files in the specified directory just like the **dir** command of DOS.

Solution

```java
import java.io.File;
public class DirSizeReport {
    public static void main(String[] args) {
        File dir = new File(args[0]);
        DirSizeReport app = new DirSizeReport();
        app.getFileReport(dir);
    }
    long getFileReport(File dir) {
        long size = 0;
        if(dir.isDirectory()) {
            String dirName = dir.getName();
            File files[] = dir.listFiles();
            for (int i = 0; i < files.length; i++) {
                size+=getFileReport(files[i]);
                System.out.println(size);
            }

                        System.out.println("Dir Name: "+dirName+", Size(bytes): "+size);
            return size;
        }else {
            String fileName = dir.getName();
                        System.out.println("File Name: "+fileName+", Size(bytes): "+dir.length());
            return dir.length();
        }
    }
}
```

Q3. Write a program that accepts names of input & output text files as command-line arguments, and copies the input file to the output file, converting all letters to the uppercase. The input file should be read using **BufferedReader** stream and contents to output file should be written using **PrintWriter** stream.

Solution

```java
import java.io.*;
public class CopyFile {
    public static void main(String[] args) throws IOException {
        String file1 = args[0];
        String file2 = args[1];
        copy(file1,file2);
    }
    static void copy(String file1, String file2) throws IOException {
        BufferedReader br = new BufferedReader(new FileReader(file1));
        PrintWriter out = new PrintWriter(file2);
        String str =  br.readLine();
        while(str != null) {
            out.println(str.toUpperCase());
            str = br.readLine();
        }
```

```
            out.close();
            br.close();
                  System.out.println(file1+" File succeffully copied in: "+file2);
      }
}
```

Q4. Write a program to input the Name, Sex, Height and Weight of n persons from the keyboard and store them in a file "height.dat".

Solution

```
import java.io.*;
public class StoreInFile {
      public static void main(String[] args) throws IOException {
            String fileName = "height.dat";
            new StoreInFile().store(fileName);
      }
      void store(String fileName) throws IOException {
                  BufferedReader br = new BufferedReader(new InputStreamReader(System.in));
            boolean isExist = false;
            if(new File(fileName).exists()) {
                  isExist = true;
            }
                  PrintWriter out = new PrintWriter(new FileWriter(fileName,true));
            String name, sex, height, weight;
            if(!isExist) {
                  out.println("Name\t\tSex\tHeight\tWeight");
            }
            String wantToExit = null;
            do {
            System.out.print("Enter Name: ");
            name = br.readLine();
            System.out.print("Enter sex: ");
            sex = br.readLine();
            System.out.print("Enter Height(in cm): ");
            height = br.readLine();
            System.out.print("Enter Weight(in kg): ");
            weight = br.readLine();
            out.println(name+"\t\t"+sex+"\t"+height+"\t"+weight);
                  System.out.println("Do you want to add more records: (Yes: Y or No: any other
                  char)");
            wantToExit = br.readLine();
            }while(wantToExit.equalsIgnoreCase("Y"));
            out.close();
            br.close();
      }
}
```

11 AWT APPLICATION

1. Intorduction

This chapter provides the knowledge for creating real time AWT-based applications. Here we provide the code for applications that are useful for better understanding of the basic concepts of AWT.

2. Simple Calculator

This calculator can perform Addition, Subtraction, Division and Multiplication operations on two values provided in the TextFields.

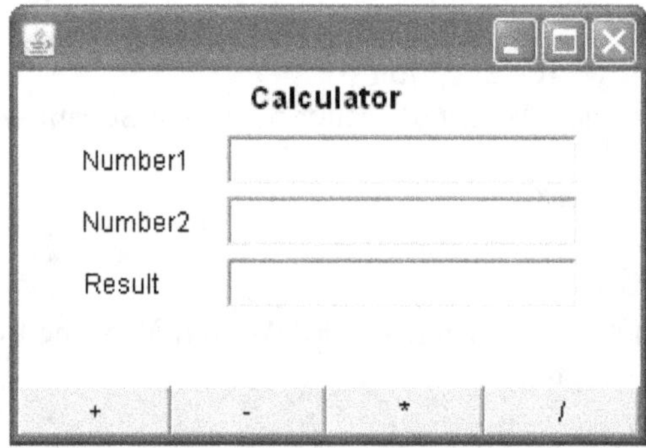


```
1  import java.awt.*;
2  import java.awt.event.*;
3  class Calculator extends Frame implements ActionListener
4  { Button badd,bsub,bmult,bdiv;
5     TextField tnum1,tnum2,tresult;
6     Label lnum1,lnum2,lresult;
7     Calculator()
8     {    Panel pcen=new Panel(new FlowLayout());
9          Panel ps=new Panel(new GridLayout(1,4));
10         lnum1=new Label("Number1");
11         lnum2=new Label("Number2");
12         lresult=new Label("Result    ");
13         tnum1=new TextField(20);
14         tnum2=new TextField(20);
15         tresult=new TextField(20);
16         badd=new Button("+");
17         bsub=new Button("-");
18         bmult=new Button("*");
19         bdiv=new Button("/");
```

```java
20      pcen.add(lnum1);
21      pcen.add(tnum1);
22      pcen.add(lnum2);
23      pcen.add(tnum2);
24      pcen.add(lresult);
25      pcen.add(tresult);
26      ps.add(badd);
27      ps.add(bsub);
28      ps.add(bmult);
29      ps.add(bdiv);
30      badd.addActionListener(this);
31      bsub.addActionListener(this);
32      bmult.addActionListener(this);
33      bdiv.addActionListener(this);
34      Label lc=new Label("Calculator",Label.CENTER);
35      lc.setFont(new Font("TimesNewRoman",Font.BOLD,14));
36      add(lc,BorderLayout.NORTH);
37      add(pcen);
38      add(ps,BorderLayout.SOUTH);
39      setBounds(100,100,300,300);
40      addWindowListener(new MyWindowListener());
41      setVisible(true);
42  }
43
44  public static void main(String args[])
45  {   Calculator f=new Calculator();
46  }
47
48  public void actionPerformed(ActionEvent ae)
49  {   if(tnum1.getText().equals(""))
50              return;
51      if(tnum2.getText().equals(""))
52              return;
53      Button but = (Button) ae.getSource();
54      double num1,num2,result;
55      num1=Double.parseDouble(tnum1.getText());
56      num2=Double.parseDouble(tnum2.getText());
57      if(but==badd)
58      {   result=num1+num2;
59          tresult.setText(String.valueOf(result));
60      }
61      else if(but==bsub)
62      {   result=num1-num2;
```

```
63              tresult.setText(String.valueOf(result));
64          }
65      else if(but==bmult)
66      {    result=num1*num2;
67              tresult.setText(String.valueOf(result));
68          }
79      else if(but==bdiv)
70      {    result=num1/num2;
71              tresult.setText(String.valueOf(result));
72          }
73  }
74 }
75
76 class MyWindowListener extends WindowAdapter
77 { public void windowClosing(WindowEvent we)
78  {     System.out.println("Window Closing");
79        Frame f = (Frame) we.getSource();
80        f.dispose();
81  }
82 }
```

3. Notepad Application

This application is a simple text editor like notepad. Only 2-3 functionalities are implemented. You can extend the application to add more features.

The Notepad and MyWindowListener Classes

```
1   class MyWindowListener extends WindowAdapter
2   { public void windowClosing(WindowEvent we)
3     {     System.out.println("Window Closing");
4           Frame f = (Frame) we.getWindow();
5           f.dispose();
6     }
7   }
```

```java
import java.awt.*;
import java.awt.event.*;
import java.io.*;
public class Notepad implements ActionListener,TextListener
{  MenuBar mbar;
   Menu file,edit,format,help;
   MenuItem fnew,open,save,saveAs,page,print,exit;
   MenuItem undo,cut,copy,paste;
   MenuItem wordwrap,font;
   MenuItem about,topics;
   TextArea ta;
   Frame f;
   boolean changeflag;

   public Notepad()
   {      f=new Frame("Notepad");
          mbar=new MenuBar();
          f.setMenuBar(mbar);
          ta=new TextArea();
          f.add(ta);
          ta.addTextListener(this);
          file=new Menu("File");
          edit=new Menu("Edit");
          format=new Menu("Format");
          help=new Menu("Help");
          fnew=new MenuItem("New");
          fnew.addActionListener(this);
          open=new MenuItem("Open");
          open.addActionListener(this);
          save=new MenuItem("Save");
          save.addActionListener(this);
          saveAs=new MenuItem("SaveAs");
          saveAs.addActionListener(this);
          page=new MenuItem("Page Setup...");
          page.addActionListener(this);
          print=new MenuItem("Print...");
          print.addActionListener(this);
          exit=new MenuItem("Exit");
          exit.addActionListener(this);
          undo=new MenuItem("Undo");
          undo.addActionListener(this);
          cut=new MenuItem("Cut");
          cut.addActionListener(this);
          copy=new MenuItem("Copy");
          copy.addActionListener(this);
          paste=new MenuItem("Paste");
          paste.addActionListener(this);
          wordwrap=new MenuItem("Word Wrap");
          wordwrap.addActionListener(this);
          font=new MenuItem("Font...");
```

```
50          font.addActionListener(this);
51          about=new MenuItem("About Notepad");
52          about.addActionListener(this);
53          topics=new MenuItem("Help topics");
54          topics.addActionListener(this);
55          file.add(fnew);
56          file.add(open);
57          file.add(save);
58          file.add(saveAs);
59          file.addSeparator();
60          file.add(page);
61          file.add(print);
62          file.addSeparator();
63          file.add(exit);
64          edit.add(undo);
65          edit.addSeparator();
66          edit.add(cut);
67          edit.add(copy);
68          edit.add(paste);
69          format.add(wordwrap);
70          format.add(font);
71          help.add(topics);
72          help.addSeparator();
73          help.add(about);
74          mbar.add(file);
75          mbar.add(edit);
76          mbar.add(format);
77          mbar.add(help);
78          f.addWindowListener(new MyWindowListener());
79          f.setBounds(100,100,600,400);
80          f.setVisible(true);
81    }

82    public static void main(String args[])
83    {     new Notepad();
84    }
85    public void actionPerformed(ActionEvent ae)
86    {     MenuItem mi=(MenuItem)ae.getSource();
87          try
88          {
89              if(mi==fnew)
90              {     ta.setText("");
91                    changeflag=false;
92              }
93              else if(mi==open)
94              {     FileDialog fd=new FileDialog(f,"OPEN",FileDialog.LOAD);
95                    fd.setVisible(true);
96                    File file=new File(fd.getDirectory()+"\\"+fd.getFile());
97                    Reader r=new BufferedReader(new FileReader(file));
98                    char ch[]=new char[(int)file.length()];
```

```
99                      r.read(ch,0,ch.length);
100                     String s=new String(ch);
101                     ta.setText(s);
102                     r.close();
103                     f.setTitle(fd.getFile()+" -Notepad");
104                     changeflag=false;
105                 }
106             else if(mi==save)
107             {   FileDialog fds=new FileDialog(f,"Save",FileDialog.SAVE);
108                 fds.setVisible(true);
109               Writer w=new FileWriter(fds.getDirectory()+"\\"+fds.getFile());
110                 String str=ta.getText();
111                 w.write(str);
112                 w.close();
113                 f.setTitle(fds.getFile()+" -Notepad");
114                 mi.setEnabled(false);
115                 changeflag=false;
116
117             }
118             else if(mi==saveAs)
119             {   FileDialog fds=new FileDialog(f,"Save",FileDialog.SAVE);
120                 fds.setVisible(true);
121               Writer w=new FileWriter(fds.getDirectory()+"\\"+fds.getFile());
122                 String str=ta.getText();
123                 w.write(str);
124                 w.close();
125                 f.setTitle(fds.getFile()+" -Notepad");
126             }
127             else if(mi==exit)
128             {   f.dispose();
129             }
130         }
131     catch(IOException e)
132         {   System.out.println(e.getMessage());
133         }
134 }
135 public void textValueChanged(TextEvent te)
136 {
137     if(!changeflag)
138     {   save.setEnabled(true);
139         changeflag = true;
140     }
141 }
142 }
```

4. Catch Me Application

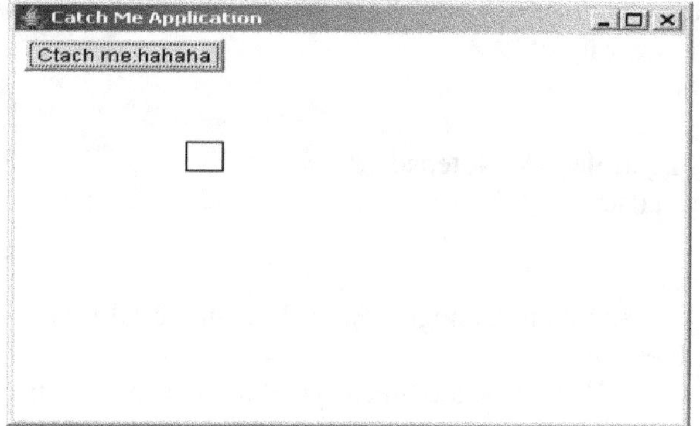

The CatchMe Class

```
1   import java.awt.*;
2   import java.awt.event.*;
3   public class CatchMe extends Frame implements MouseListener, MouseMotionListener
4   {  String msg="";
5      int mx=0,my=0;
6      int x=100,y=100;
7      int x1,y1,w1,h1;
8      Button b;
9      CatchMe()
10  {     setTitle("Catch Me Application");
11        setLayout(new FlowLayout());
12        b=new Button("Ctach me:hahaha");
13        b.addMouseListener(this);
14        addMouseMotionListener(this);
15        add(b);
16        setExtendedState(Frame.MAXIMIZED_BOTH);
17        setVisible(true);
18  }
19  public void mouseEntered(MouseEvent me)
20  {     mx=me.getX();
21        my=me.getY();
22        x1=b.getX();   //get Location of the button
23        y1=b.getY();
24        w1=b.getWidth();
25        h1=b.getHeight();
26        int n1=(int)(Math.random()*100);
27        int n2=(int)(Math.random()*100);
28        b.setLocation(100+(x1+n1)%600,100+(y1+n2)%450);
29  }
30  public void mouseClicked(MouseEvent me)
31  {
32  }
33  public void mouseExited(MouseEvent me)
34  {
35  }
36  public void mousePressed(MouseEvent me)
```

```
37   {
38   }
39   public void mouseReleased(MouseEvent me)
40   {
41   }
42   public  void paint(Graphics g)
43   {
44        g.drawRect(x,y,20,20);
45   }
46   public static void main(String args[])
47   {    CatchMe ml=new CatchMe();
48   }
49
50   public void mouseDragged(MouseEvent me){}
51   public void mouseMoved(MouseEvent me)
52   {    //Used for catching the rectangle drawn in the paint method
53        mx=me.getX();
54        my=me.getY();
55        if((mx>=x-10) && (mx<=x+30) && (my>=y-10) && (my<=y+30))
56        {    int n1=(int)(Math.random()*100);
57             int n2=(int)(Math.random()*100);
58             x=100+(x+n1)%600;
59             y=100+(y+n2)%450;
60             repaint();
61        }
62
63   }
64 }
```

5. Painting Application

```
1   import java.awt.*;
2   import java.awt.event.*;
3   import java.io.*;
4   public class PaintingDrag1 extends Frame implements MouseListener,
5   WindowListener, MouseMotionListener,ActionListener,ItemListener
6   { int dragX,dragY,preX,preY,moveX,moveY,releX,releY;
7       Button bPencil,brect,boval,bline, bref,but;
8       String command;
9       Choice c;
10   Color color=Color.green;
11
12   public PaintingDrag1()
13   {
14        bPencil=new Button("Pencil");
15        boval=new Button("Oval");
16        brect=new Button("Rectangle");
17        bline=new Button("Line");
18        bref=new Button("Refresh");
```

```java
19        c=new Choice();
20        c.add("Red");
21        c.add("Green");
22        c.add("Blue");
23        c.add("Black");
24        c.add("Gray");
25        c.addItemListener(this);
26        c.select("Green");
27        bPencil.addActionListener(this);
28        boval.addActionListener(this);
29        brect.addActionListener(this);
39        bline.addActionListener(this);
31        bref.addActionListener(this);
32        Panel pb=new Panel(new FlowLayout(FlowLayout.LEFT));
33        pb.setBackground(Color.lightGray);
34        pb.add(bPencil);
35        pb.add(boval);
36        pb.add(brect);
37        pb.add(bline);
38        pb.add(bref);
39        pb.add(c);
40        add(pb,BorderLayout.NORTH);
41        setBounds(100,100,500,500);
42        setBackground(Color.white);
43        addMouseListener(this);
44        addWindowListener(this);
45        addMouseMotionListener(this);
46        setVisible(true);
47   }
48
49   public static void main(String args[])
50   {    PaintingDrag1 f=new PaintingDrag1();
51   }
52
53   public void paint(Graphics g)
54   {    if(command==null)
55            return;
56        if(command.equals("Pencil"))
57        {    g.setColor(color);
58             g.drawLine(preX,preY,dragX,dragY);
59             preX=dragX;
60             preY=dragY;
61        }
```

```
62        if(command.equals("Oval"))
63    {    g.setColor(color);
64         int w=releX-preX;
65         int x=0;
66         if(w<0)
67         {    w=-w;
68              x=releX;
69         }
70         else
71         {    x=preX;
72         }
73         int h=releY-preY;
74         int y=0;
75         if(h<0)
76         {    h=-h;
77              y=releY;
78         }
79         else
80         {    y=preY;
81         }
82         g.drawOval(x,y,w,h);
83    }
84        if(command.equals("Rectangle"))
85    {    g.setColor(color);
86         int w=releX-preX;
87         int x=0;
88         if(w<0)
89         {    w=-w;
90              x=releX;
91         }
92         else
93         {    x=preX;
94         }
95         int h=releY-preY;
96         int y=0;
97         if(h<0)
98         {    h=-h;
99                  y=releY;
100        }
101        else
102        {    y=preY;
103        }
104        g.drawRect(x,y,w,h);
```

```
105         }
106         if(command.equals("Line"))
107         {    g.setColor(color);
108              g.drawLine(preX,preY,releX,releY);
109         }
110         if(command.equals("Refresh"))
111         {    g.setColor(color);
112              g.clearRect(0,0,1000,1000);
113         }
114 }
115
116 public void update(Graphics g)
117 {
118      paint(g);
119 }
120
121 //implementing MouseListener's methods
122 public void mouseClicked(MouseEvent me)
123 {
124 }
125
126 public void mouseEntered(MouseEvent me)
127 {
128 }
129
130 public void mouseExited(MouseEvent me)
131 {
132 }
133
134 public void mousePressed(MouseEvent me)
135 {    preX=me.getX();
136      preY=me.getY();
137 }
138
139 public void mouseReleased(MouseEvent me)
140 {    releX=me.getX();
141      releY=me.getY();
142      if(command==null)
143          return;
144      if(command.equals("Oval"))
145          repaint();
146      if(command.equals("Rectangle"))
147          repaint();
```

```
148     if(command.equals("Line"))
149          repaint();
150 }
151 //Implementing WindowListeners's methods
152 public void windowOpened(WindowEvent we)
153 {
154 }
155
156 public void windowActivated(WindowEvent we)
157 {
158 }
159
160 public void windowClosing(WindowEvent we)
161 {    Frame f=(Frame)we.getSource();
162      dispose();
163 }
164
165 public void windowIconified(WindowEvent we)
166 {    command=null;
167 }
168
169 public void windowDeiconified(WindowEvent we)
170 {
171 }
172
173 public void windowClosed(WindowEvent we)
174 {
175 }
176
177 public void windowDeactivated(WindowEvent we)
178 {
179 }
180
181 //implementing MouseMotionListener
182 public void mouseDragged(MouseEvent me)
183 {    dragX=me.getX();
184      dragY=me.getY();
185      if(command==null)
186           return;
187      if(command.equals("Pencil"))
188           repaint();
189 }
190
```

```
191  public void mouseMoved(MouseEvent me)
192  {     moveX=me.getX();
193        moveY=me.getY();
194  }
195
196  //implementing ActionListener
197  public void actionPerformed(ActionEvent ae)
198  {     but=(Button)ae.getSource();
199        command=but.getActionCommand();
200        preX=0;preY=0;
201        releX=0;releY=0;dragX=0;dragY=0;
202        moveX=0;moveY=0;
203        if(command.equals("Refresh"));
204        {     repaint();
205        }
206  }
207  //implementing ItemListener
208  public void itemStateChanged(ItemEvent ie)
209  {     String item=(String)ie.getItem();
210        but.requestFocus();
211        if(item.equals("Red"))
212        {     color=Color.red;
213        }
214        else if(item.equals("Green"))
215        {     color=Color.green;
216        }
217        else if(item.equals("Blue"))
218        {     color=Color.blue;
219        }
220        else if(item.equals("Gray"))
221        {     color=Color.gray;
222        }
223        else if(item.equals("Black"))
224        {     color=Color.black;
225        }
226  }
227  }
```

6. GridBagLayout (A Layout Manager)

This Layout holds the characteristics of both the FlowLayout (component takes its preferred size) and GridLayout (component is added in particular grid). The **GridBagLayout** class is a flexible layout manager that aligns components vertically and horizontally, without requiring that the components be of the same size. This Layout Manager has the following characteristics:

- **Complex layout facilities can be placed in a grid.**
- **A single component can take its preferred size.**
- **A component can extend over more than one cell.**

To layout complex GUI in **GridBagLayout** some constraints (insets, x and y positioning, grid width, grid height, etc.) can be imposed by the use of a Class **GridBagConstraints**. This class includes many fields to specify the constraints, which can be used to position any component.

To use a grid bag layout effectively, you must customize one or more of the **GridBagConstraints** objects that are associated with its components. You customize a **GridBagConstraints** object by setting one or more of its instance variables:

6.1 The gridx and gridy Constraints
Specifies the cell containing the leading corner of the component's display area, where the cell at the origin of the grid has address gridx = 0, gridy = 0. For horizontal left-to-right layout, a component's leading corner is its upper left.

6.2 The gridwidth and gridheight Constraints
Specifies the number of cells in a row (**gridwidth**) or column (**gridheight**) in the component's display area. The default value is 1.

6.3 The fill Constraint
Used when the component's display area is larger than the component's requested size to determine whether (and how) to resize the component. Possible values are **GridBagConstraints.NONE** (the default), **GridBagConstraints.HORIZONTAL** (make the component wide enough to fill its display area horizontally, but don't change its height), **GridBagConstraints.VERTICAL** (make the component tall enough to fill its display area vertically, but don't change its width), and **GridBagConstraints.BOTH** (make the component fill its display area entirely).

6.4 The ipadx and ipady Constraints
Specifies the component's internal padding within the layout, how much to add to the minimum size of the component. The width of the component will be at least its minimum width plus **ipadx** pixels. Similarly, the height of the component will be at least the minimum height plus **ipady** pixels.

6.5 The insets Constraint
Specifies the component's external padding, the minimum amount of space between the component and the edges of its display area.

6.6 The anchor Constraint

Used when the component is smaller than its display area to determine where (within the display area) to place the component.

- GridBagConstraints.NORTH
- GridBagConstraints.SOUTH
- GridBagConstraints.WEST
- GridBagConstraints.EAST
- GridBagConstraints.NORTHWEST
- GridBagConstraints.NORTHEAST
- GridBagConstraints.SOUTHWEST
- GridBagConstraints.SOUTHEAST
- GridBagConstraints.CENTER (the default)

6.7 The weightx and weighty Constraints

Used to determine how to distribute space, which is important for specifying resizing behavior. Unless you specify a weight for at least one component in a row (**weightx**) and column (**weighty**), all the components clump together in the center of their container. This is because when the weight is zero (the default), the **GridBagLayout** object puts any extra space between its grid of cells and the edges of the container.

Example: Design the Complaint Form as shown below:

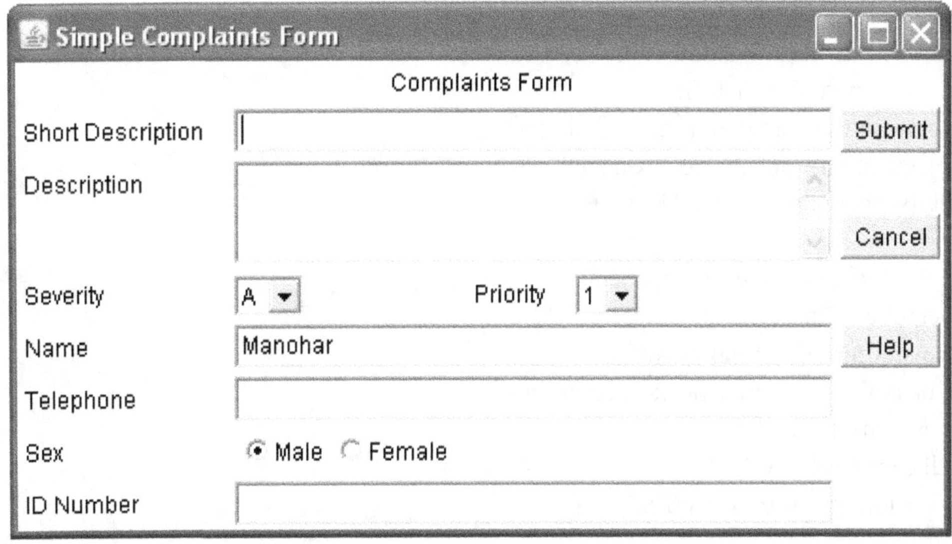


```
1   /* Using GridBagConstraints*/
2   import java.awt.*;
3   class ComplaintsForm extends Frame
4   { public  ComplaintsForm()
5     {     setTitle("Simple Complaints Form");
6           setSize(500,300);
7           Label lbl1 = new Label("Short Description");
```

```
8         TextField txt1 = new TextField();
9         Label lbl2 = new Label("Description");
10        TextArea area1 = new TextArea();
11        Label lbl3 = new Label("Severity");
12        Choice combo3 = new Choice();
13        combo3.addItem("A");
14        combo3.addItem("B");
15        combo3.addItem("C");
16        combo3.addItem("D");
17        combo3.addItem("E");
18        Label lbl4 = new Label("Priority");
19        Choice combo4 = new Choice();
20        combo4.addItem("1");
21        combo4.addItem("2");
22        combo4.addItem("3");
23        combo4.addItem("4");
24        combo4.addItem("5");
25        Label lbl5 = new Label("Name");
26        TextField txt5 = new TextField("Manohar");
27        Label lbl6 = new Label("Telephone");
28        TextField txt6 = new TextField();
29        Label lbl7 = new Label("Sex");
30        Label lbl8 = new Label("ID Number");
31        TextField txt8 = new TextField();
32        Button submitButton = new Button("Submit");
33        Button cancelButton = new Button("Cancel");
34        Button helpButton = new Button("Help");
35
36        //Create a Panel to hold all the components
37        Panel panel = new Panel();
38        panel.setLayout(new GridBagLayout());
39        GridBagConstraints c = new GridBagConstraints();
40        c.insets = new Insets(2,2,2,2);
41        //anchor all components WEST
42        c.anchor = GridBagConstraints.WEST;
43        c.gridx = 0;
44        c.gridy = 0;
45        panel.add(lbl1,c);
46
47        c.gridx = 1;
48        c.weightx = 1.0; //Use all available horizontal space
49        c.gridwidth = 3;
50        c.fill = GridBagConstraints.HORIZONTAL; //fills the three columns
```

```java
51          panel.add(txt1,c);
52
53          c.gridwidth = 1;
54          c.gridx = 0;
55          c.gridy = 1;
56          c.weightx = 0.0; //Do not use any extra horizontal space
57          panel.add(lbl2,c);
58
59          c.gridwidth = 3;
60          c.gridheight = 2;
61          c.gridx = 1;
62          c.weightx = 1.0; //use all abailable horizontal space
63          c.weighty = 1.0; //use all abailable vertical space
64          c.fill = GridBagConstraints.BOTH;
65          panel.add(area1,c);
66
67          c.gridwidth = 1;
68          c.gridheight = 1;
69          c.gridx = 0;
70          c.gridy = 3;
71          c.weightx = 0; //Do not use any extra horizontal space
72          c.weighty = 0;
73          c.fill = GridBagConstraints.NONE;
74          panel.add(lbl3,c);
75
76          c.gridx = 1;
77          panel.add(combo3,c);
78
79          c.gridx = 2;
80          panel.add(lbl4,c);
81
82          c.gridx = 3;
83          panel.add(combo4,c);
84
85          c.gridx = 0;
86          c.gridy = 4;
87          panel.add(lbl5,c);
88
89          c.gridx = 1;
90          c.gridwidth = 3;
91          c.fill = GridBagConstraints.HORIZONTAL; //fills the three columns
92          panel.add(txt5,c);
93
```

```
94          c.gridwidth = 1;
95          c.gridx = 0;
96          c.gridy = 5;
97          panel.add(lbl6,c);
98
99          c.gridx = 1;
100         c.gridwidth = 3;
101         panel.add(txt6,c);
102
103         c.gridwidth = 1;
104         c.gridx = 0;
105         c.gridy = 6;
106         panel.add(lbl7,c);
107
108             Panel radioPanel = new Panel();
109             radioPanel.setLayout(new FlowLayout(FlowLayout.LEFT,5,0));
110             CheckboxGroup group = new CheckboxGroup();
111             Checkbox radio1 = new Checkbox("Male",group,true);
112             Checkbox radio2 = new Checkbox("Female",group,false);
113             radioPanel.add(radio1);
114             radioPanel.add(radio2);
115
116         c.gridx = 1;
117         panel.add(radioPanel,c);
118
119         c.gridx = 0;
120         c.gridy = 7;
121         panel.add(lbl8,c);
122
123         c.gridx = 1;
124         c.gridwidth = 3;
125         panel.add(txt8,c);
126
127         //adding buttons
128         c.gridx = 4;
129         c.gridy = 0;
130         panel.add(submitButton,c);
131
132         c.gridy = 2;
133         panel.add(cancelButton,c);
134
135         c.gridy = 4;
136         panel.add(helpButton,c);
```

```
137       this.add(panel);
138       Label heading = new Label("Complaints Form", Label.CENTER);
139       this .add(heading,BorderLayout.NORTH);
140       setVisible(true);
141 }
142 public static void main(String args[])
143 {     ComplaintsForm cl = new  ComplaintsForm();
144 }
145 }
```

ABOUT THE AUTHOR

Dr T.N.Sharma has more than16 years of experience in various areas of IT. He has good experience of software development, teaching and training.He has taught a lots of subjects of IT at various levels. Apart from all other his work, he is teaching Java from last about 15 years. He has published a lots of papers and books.

This books Is written by keeping in mind the popularity of java as one of the most famous general purpose programming language which are being taught in almost all the computer related studies like BCA, MCA, B.Tech etc. A number of books are available in the market for learning the aspects of java. This book is written exclusively for programming problems. Programming problems for different topics of core java are collected and presented in this book. A good combination of solved and unsolved programming questions are given here. Readers are expected to solve the unsolved questions of their own. Even if, they feel any trouble, the can contact the authors on mail id tnsharma@logicpace.com and logicpace@gmail.com.

Learn Java by Examples